INNER CHILD HEALING - AN ENCOUNTER WITH SELF

CULTIVATING FORGIVENESS AS A BRIDGE TO HEALING PAST WOUNDS AND NURTURING THE INNER CHILD

JANET G CRUZ

For permissions requests, speaking inquiries, and bulk order purchase options, email: publishing@uconcept.com.

ISBN: 978-1-960188-40-3 | E-book

ISBN: 978-1-960188-41-0 | Paperback

ISBN: 978-1-960188-42-7 | Hardcover

Published by Unlimited Concepts, Coconut Creek, Florida.

www.publishing.uconcept.com

Book, Editing, and Cover Design by Janet M Garcia | UConceptDesigns.com

Published in the United States of America.

I want to dedicate this book to everyone, including myself, as we all carry baggage from our childhood that will continue to affect our lives today if not resolved.

I hope that after reading these pages you will soon be able to put into practice the exercises shared in the book so that you can immediately begin the process of your inner child healing and live a fulfilling life.

CONTENTS

INTRODUCTION

One night, I sat in my study thinking about my life as I looked at some photos, and came across a picture of myself as a kid which brought back a flood of emotions to me, even tears, and a sudden realization hit me hard at that moment when I saw that young child in one of the photo who seemed both distant and yet so familiar to me, made me realize how my current struggles are linked to unresolved pain from my childhood days. This revelation sparked my path towards researching and learning about the importance of inner child healing, which in turn led me to study Psychology and Sociology as I really wanted to understand human behavior. It is this blend of professional expertise and personal passion that I bring to you through this book.

The purpose of this book is simple yet profound: to help you uncover and understand the traumas of your past that still prevent you from living your life fully. Through this understanding, you can begin the journey towards forgiveness and a happier life. Inner child healing is crucial as it is the foundation for emotional well-being. When we heal our inner child, we heal our past and open the door to a brighter future.

Healing our inner child entails recognizing and dealing with the needs and traumas from our past that were left unmet or unresolved during childhood years – experiences that greatly influence our beliefs and actions as grown ups in how we respond emotionally to situations. Studies indicate that unaddressed childhood traumas can lead to a range of mental challenges such as anxiety and depression while also impacting our interactions within relationships. Through the process of inner child healing therapy or practices aimed at nurturing this aspect of ourselves from the past can help us break free from negative patterns and prepare the way for a more meaningful and satisfying life.

Here's a personal story I'd like to share with you about Sarah who was dealing with feelings of not being good enough (unworthiness) and fear of being left alone (abandonment), which stemmed from her experiences as a child. Through therapy, she was able to address these feelings of being neglected and unseen, and showed her a new perspective. As a result, she started building her self-worth by addressing those traumas from the past and taking care of her inner child, which in turn lead her to establish healthier connections with other people. Sarah's story motivated me to explore more about the significance of inner child healing.

I have structured this book to guide you through your own healing journey. In the first chapter, I'll talk about the concept of the inner child and its impact on our adult lives. The subsequent chapters will examine specific traumas and how they manifest in adulthood. Each chapter will build on the previous one, providing you with tools and exercises that can help you in the healing process. We will cover topics such as self-compassion, forgiveness, and building healthy relationships. By the end of the book, you will have a comprehensive understanding of your inner child and the steps needed to nurture and heal.

I encourage you to engage with this journey because revitalizing your authentic self has the potential to completely change your life in ways you might not even realize yet. You have the ability to liberate yourself from constraints and shape a future brimming with happiness, love, and contentment. This path won't be simple and easy, but I promise you that it'll be worthwhile. You have every right to lead a life unburdened by the shadows of your past. You deserve to find peace and happiness.

Remember, this book is not just about understanding your past, but also about embracing your future. By healing, you are taking the first step towards a life of emotional freedom. So, take a deep breath, open your heart, and let's begin this journey together. The path to healing awaits you, and I am honored to walk it with you.

UNDERSTANDING YOUR INNER CHILD

*a*s a child, I used to feel like nobody really got me. I was kind of alone even with people around me who cared. I grew up shy. It took me a while to figure out why I felt that way. I recall this one session of couples therapy when the therapist told me to look at my earliest memories and write down a letter to "my younger self." In that moment, all these emotions came flooding out of me that I hadn't realized were still there. This activity brought to light the child within me that carries old wounds, and made me realize that my current challenges were linked to unresolved events from my childhood days.This realization marked the beginning of a path towards nurturing and healing my inner child.

UNCOVERING YOUR INNER CHILD

The notion of the 'inner child' is a concept in psychology that has been extensively studied on a psychological level over time. It represents the element of an individual's personality that emerges before entering adolescence.This part of our identity encapsulates our upbringing and life experiences. It's often seen as a somewhat separate entity within us that retains our earliest recollections and emotions along with unfulfilled aspirations. This phrase became popular within therapy circles due to pioneers such as John Bradshaw who emphasized the influence of childhood encounters on our adult lives. Lucia Capacchione's contributions to art therapy and journal writing have introduced techniques for nurturing your inner child—a practice now embraced in both thera-peutic and healthcare environments alike. As an artist myself, I view painting as a portal to a refuge or sanctuary where I can immerse myself for hours, engaging in my creative expression and profound reflection simultaneously.

Various psychological theories that back the concept of child work offer a wide range of viewpoints and methods to explore this idea further. Carl Jung introduced the notion of the inner child as a significant element of the psyche repre-senting purity and imagination with the potential for growth and advancement. In Roberto Assagioli's Psychosynthesis theory, the inner child is viewed as a persona that contributes to achieving completeness when fused seamlessly with the mature self. In Internal Family Systems (IFS), Richard Schwartz suggests that we all have hidden inner child sub personalities known as "exiles" that often function without our knowledge. A central idea stresses the significance of recognizing and nurturing these inner child parts to enhance our overall well being.

Understanding the importance of acknowledging our inner child is key in dealing with our emotional and mental challenges in a meaningful way as adults. It's important not to overlook this aspect of ourselves as it prevents us from addressing wounds and carrying emotional baggage into our grown up years. Reconnecting with the innocence and curiosity of our inner child offers us a chance to show ourselves the love and empathy that may have been lacking in our early years. This approach paves the way to attaining freedom and living a fulfilling and rewarding life.

As we become adults, our inner child still shows itself in the way we behave and feel based on our childhood experiences that continue to influence us throughout our lives. For example if you were constantly criticized as a child you might find it hard to deal with situations where you feel like you need to be perfect and fear making mistakes as an adult. Moreover, the emotional responses we have can also be tied to hurts and wounds from those earlier times in our lives. These responses are frequently connected to lasting feelings from your childhood.

Difficulties in relationships and building relationships can also be linked to experiences that have caused emotional pain during our younger years. If you've felt abandoned or neglected in the past, it may lead to difficulty trusting others and fear of abandonment resurfacing. These challenges might result in a scenario where you seek reassurance and emotional support from others (co-dependency). It's crucial to identify these patterns in order to break free from recurring cycles and cultivate happier relationships.

Take a moment to pause and connect with your inner child by trying a guided visualization exercise. Locate a quiet place where you can unwind without any interruptions and sit comfortably with your eyes closed. Breathe deeply to center yourself and envision a setting where you feel completely at ease. Whether it's a serene beach or a lush forest or even a cozy room. Picture yourself as a child, in that environment, joyfully exploring and playing without any concerns. When you feel ready and comfortable, take the time to connect with your inner child. Take the opportunity to observe the reactions closely and gain a deeper understanding of its emotions and needs by engaging in a comforting conversation with your inner child without any judgment or criticism present during this interaction. After completing this reflection session, take a moment to write down your thoughts, about the experience and consider the insights gained from connecting with your inner child and how it affected you emotionally.

Signs of a hurt inner child commonly involve feelings of not being good enough and deserving of love, and fear of being left behind or rejected as well as having trouble relying on others. Traces of these behaviors usually link back to needs and unresolved past hurts from your childhood. If you find yourself grappling with feelings of inadequacy, you might look for approval from others while questioning your own capabilities.The fear of being abandoned could lead you to either become overly attached, or push people away to shield yourself from pain. Difficulty in trusting others often leads to creating emotional distance even with those who genuinely care about you and recognizing these characteristics is the step towards recovery and healing.

To start the healing journey, you need to overcome those past wounds that hinder your growth and progress as a person, and it involves understanding and tending to the inner child within you with patience and kindness while confronting challenging feelings bravely. Always remember that you are not walking this path alone; many individuals have trodden this road before and discovered peace and contentment at the end of it all. Embracing the possibility of breaking from past struggles opens up the potential to lead a life overflowing with happiness and self love.

THE EMOTIONAL BAGGAGE WE CARRY

Carrying baggage means holding onto unresolved feelings and past experiences that affect how we live today. These emotions often stem from childhood and may involve guilt, shame, and fear. It's like dragging a backpack loaded with past pain and unfulfilled desires. Think about running a marathon with that weight on your back; it would definitely slow you down and make the journey harder. In the way, that emotional baggage hinders us from fully embracing life. Emotions can come from experiences like receiving negative feedback from parents or facing bullying in school, or going through traumatic events that affect us deeply and stay with us for a while, shaping how we think and behave in our interactions with others.

Bringing emotional burdens into our adult lives can deeply impact us in various ways as we navigate relationships and interactions with others over time. For instance, unresolved childhood guilt may lead to apologizing for things that may not even be our fault. This behavior can create an uneven dynamic in relationships. Feelings of shame may cause us to believe that we are undeserving of love which could result in self sabotage tendencies and push people away from us. On the other hand, being consumed by fear might make us overly cautious and hesitant in forming meaningful connections with others. In a professional environment, emotional burdens can affect your trajectory and choices at work. Feeling guilty may result in you overcommitting and experiencing burnout. Experiencing shame might cause you to question your skills leading you to miss out on chances for progress. Feeling afraid could immobilize you, stopping you from pursuing opportunities that could foster both personal and career development.

You can use the questions to explore how your past experiences have shaped your current situation: Do you often doubt your worthiness of love or success? Do you catch yourself dwelling on mistakes? Are there situations that make you feel anxious and prompt you to avoid them? These inquiries can assist you in discovering the burdens you may be carrying with you day by day. You can find some self-assessment tools at:

https://www.thoughtfulleader.com/self-assessment-tools/

After acknowledging and understanding your burdens and baggage, it's crucial to let them go to embark on the healing journey effectively. That process involves shedding emotions that no longer benefit you by expressing them through writing in a journal. This practice enables you to gain clarity and deeper understanding of your feelings and experiences. Expressive writing allows you to release trapped emotions while making sense of your history. Additionally, mindfulness exercises and meditation can further aid in this release process. These methods will help you focus on the moment and examine your thoughts without criticism or evaluation. They will allow you to have an environment to work through and let go of emotions in a positive manner. Scheduling therapy or counseling sessions is also another effective approach. A skilled therapist can lead you in navigating the release process and offer assistance and techniques customized to your specific requirements.

Let me share Emily's story. She had a time dealing with emotional baggage from her childhood due to a critical parent who constantly criticized her flaws while growing up. As an adult today, Emily faces challenges with self confidence and a fear of not succeeding in life. She tends to find herself in relationships where she feels undervalued and inadequate. Through therapy, she's slowly working through her emotional burdens. One of the strategies she uses is writing letters to comfort herself with the love and support she missed out back then. Emily focused on being present in the moment and paying attention to how her body responded to challenging moments of dwelling on them endlessly in her mind. She gradually let go of the burden of guilt and shame she carried, learned to establish boundaries and put her well-being first. As a result, her connections with others became stronger and she became more daring in pursuing opportunities in both, her personal life and professional endeavors, resulting in significant personal growth.

By recognizing and letting go of your baggage you can liberate yourself from the weight of past experiences. This journey demands patience and kindness toward yourself but the benefits are significant. You will discover you better equipped to cultivate connections, make decisive choices and lead a life that resonates with your authentic self. Keep in mind the burdens you bear do not shape who you are. You possess the ability to unpack them and embrace life to the fullest.

RECOGNIZING CHILDHOOD WOUNDS

Growing up leaves lasting marks that can influentially guide our lives as grown ups in ways that are deeply felt but not visible to the naked eye. Emotional neglect is a significant wound that is often overlooked. It happens when a child's emotional needs are habitually overlooked resulting in feelings of insignificance and invisibility. The absence of emotional encouragement can trigger feelings of low self-esteem and a persistent belief in one's lack of worth. As grown ups, these individuals may find it challenging to feel good about themselves relying heavily upon external validation to fill the emptiness left from unmet childhood longings.

It could be challenging for them to communicate their feelings effectively which may result in increased loneliness and miscommunication within their relationships.

One of the scars from childhood is the fear of abandonment, which usually arises when a child's primary caregiver is physically or emotionally unavailable in some way. This fear can lead to an anxiety about being abandoned or rejected. Children who face abandonment issues might either become overly dependent or distant emotionally as they try to shield themselves from pain. These behaviors often carry over into adulthood and can impact their capacity to build and sustain meaningful relationships. In order to prevent the possibility of being left alone and isolated from others, people might distance themselves from others or become excessively dependent on them, ultimately leading to the breakdown of those relationships.

Physical and emotional abuse can result in wounds as well as deep emotional effects that are hard to heal from. In cases of abuse, survivors might constantly feel the need to be alert and vigilant, even in seemingly safe situations. Emotional abuse involving attacks and ongoing criticism can erode a child's self-esteem causing long term anxiety and a skewed self-perception. People who have experienced mistreatment may battle feelings of inadequacy and believe they are unworthy or destined to be treated poorly. This could lead to a pattern of harmful relationships or self-destructive actions.

In adulthood, you might see how emotional scars from childhood show up in different ways, like having a fear of getting close to others and showing your true feelings easily. Those who were not emotionally supported or felt abandoned when young often put up walls to shield themselves from getting hurt. They're afraid of opening up and facing rejection or pain. This fear stops them from building relationships that mean something to them; instead, they feel lonely and unsatisfied. Also, some people try to make up from feeling 'not enough' in some way—by pushing themselves in everything they do—trying to prove their worth, through their achievements. Sometimes, when people pursue success at all costs and strive to demonstrate their value, it can take a toll on their emotional health in the long run.

Chronic anxiety and tension often affect people who have experienced childhood difficulties. The lingering feelings and past hurts result in a sense of unease that hinders relaxation and inner calmness. This can lead to ailments such as headaches, sleep disturbances, and digestive problems that worsen their overall well-being. The mind remains constantly vigilant, constantly anticipating challenges ahead. This constant state of readiness can be draining and overwhelming.

Think about Tom's situation—he had a time with feelings of abandonment because his dad left when he was young. As a grown up, Tom struggled to believe in people and was always worried they would leave him as well. This fear made him stick to shallow relationships because he would rather end things than get too close and risk being hurt. With therapy, Tom started to see this pattern, how it linked back to his childhood. He focused on trusting others and being open to making more meaningful relationships through that effort.

Lisa is an example of someone who went through emotional neglect in her childhood days—feeling like she was always invisible, and her emotions and desires overlooked due to her parents busy schedules. As she grew older and entered adult-hood, Lisa struggled with issues related to self-esteem and a fear of rejection. This led her to end up in relationships where her needs were often ignored or unmet, thus creating a cycle of neglect. With the support and guidance of a therapist, Lisa started working on self love and assertiveness techniques to prioritize her needs and establish healthy boundaries for herself.

Healing childhood wounds requires a variety of approaches to address them, such as engaging in inner child dialogues and practicing reparenting techniques which involve providing the love and support that may have been missing during childhood years. By having conversations with your inner child and embodying the role of a nurturing and protective parent figure for them can be beneficial in this healing process. Additionally, Cognitive Behavioral Therapy (CBT) exercises play a role in challenging and reshaping negative beliefs and thought patterns that have roots in childhood experiences. These exercises aim to replace thoughts with more positive and empowering ones to promote healing. Same as contemplative prayer.

Creating a support system is also essential for the healing journey. Having compassionate people around you can offer the emotional support necessary to confront and recover from previous traumas. This could involve friends or family members as well as participation in support groups or seeking professional help from a therapist. Opening up about your experiences and receiving empathy can be comforting and promote healing. Recovering from childhood traumas and hurts is a process that demands patience and self kindness. It entails acknowledging the pain you have endured, recognizing its effects on you and actively working to nurture and heal your inner child. Although the path may present obstacles along the way, the satisfaction of attaining liberation and fulfillment makes it all worthwhile.

THE ROLE OF THE INNER CHILD IN ADULT LIFE

Our childhood experiences have an impact in shaping how we make decisions. The problem is that when we're making choices, it's possible that our past emotional needs and unresolved feelings from our childhood are the ones guiding us in ways we may not be fully aware of. These decision making habits are often connected to our past experiences. For example, if you were raised in an environment where your viewpoints were ignored, chances aer that as an adult, you might find it challenging to speak up for yourself and choose to stay quiet to avoid any kind of confrontation. Decisions driven by fear are frequently linked to childhood trauma as opposed to love centered decisions, which stem from self-assurance and faith in oneself for making choices that align with personal values and true identity. These behavioral patterns may influence many facets of life such as career paths and relationships on a broader scale. For example, a person who experienced neglect during childhood could potentially push themselves hard in their profession as a way to seek validation through accomplishments. In contrast, someone who has had a steady stream of support may confidently follow their passions with the belief that they deserve to achieve success.

Our relationships can be greatly influenced by our childhood too.This can lead to issues like codependency and enmeshment that stem from our childhood experiences. Codependency involves relying too much emotionally and seeking validation excessively from another person, resulting in imbalanced relationships where one person may neglect their own needs. Enmeshment happens when personal boundaries become blurred and the individuals become overly involved in each others lives. These behaviors often mirror dynamics from childhood family settings where roles and boundaries were unclear or unhealthy. Trust issues and emotional unavailability are also ways in which the inner child impacts relationships. If your trust was shattered during childhood, it could make it tough for you to open up and trust others. You might fear being let down or pushed away leading to distancing yourself emotionally to shield yourself from possible pain.

To nurture a bond with your inner child and enhance emotional control capabilities, try integrating daily self-assessments into your daily routine. Allocate a period of time each day to relax and connect with your inner child. Inquire about your inner child's emotions and desires during this time. This simple habit will aid you in fostering closeness and empathy. Using affirmations for self-comfort daily can also be beneficial for you. Develop affirmations that align with your inner child, like: " I deserve love and appreciation." Throughout the day, keep repeating these statements to strengthen your beliefs in a positive way; and, to have immediate relief when you feel distressed, comfort yourself with self-soothing techniques or give yourself a gentle hug. Visualization activities work too. Just picture a safe and caring place where your inner child is cherished and secure. Take a few minutes to visualize yourself providing comfort and encouragement to your inner child in this peaceful setting.

Reparenting is an approach to healing and nurturing the inner child by stepping into the role of a caring and supportive parent for your inner self and meeting their emotional needs with love and empathy. The process of reparenting includes several steps. Fist, acknowledging and validating the feelings and experiences of your inner child to let it know that its emotions are recognized and significant; then offering the affectionate support and guidance it requires. Consider offering words of reassurance or showing love through acts of kindness or by cherishing moments spent together in your thoughts. Imagine establishing healthy limits and a structured routine akin to a caring caregiver who offers direction and sets boundaries to foster a secure and stable atmosphere for the child within you (inner child).

Some behaviors associated with reparenting involve talking to your inner child in a compassionate and empathetic manner and providing comfort in challenging moments while promoting emotional expression without concern for criticism or judgment. A practical approach to initiate reparenting is by composing a letter addressed to your inner child where you convey affection and dedication to its welfare and assure it of your support and care. One way to go about it is to establish a routine like reading a bedtime story or doing a soothing activity such as drawing or listening to calming music. It's these gestures of kindness that can really make a difference in how secure and valued our inner child feels.

The impact of our inner child on our grown up lives is clear and proven. As we acknowledge and deal with this impact head on, it allows us to be more mindful in our choices for better connections and will lead a more genuine existence. Engaging in check-ins and affirmations while exploring self-soothing methods and visualization exercises can significantly aid in nurturing and healing our inner child effectively and practically. By incorporating these practices into our routine with a focus on reparenting ourselves as needed, we also establish a strong groundwork of self-love and emotional wellness that ultimately enhances the quality of our lives.

IDENTIFYING UNRESOLVED TRAUMA

*P*icture yourself in a city with all its hustle and bustle and all the noise and commotion surrounding you. You start to feel anxious – your heart is pounding and your palms are getting clammy. It's hard to explain the cause of this uneasiness filling you up, but it's there, it's real. This kind of feeling is something people face daily when they're carrying around traumas that are still unresolved. Those experiences can leave deep marks on our minds and bodies, whether they come from childhood trauma or from more recent events. Signs of trauma can often show up in ways that will impact our everyday routines significantly. For this reason, it's important to acknowledge and deal with them as soon as possible.

SIGNS OF UNRESOLVED TRAUMA

Unresolved past experiences can show up through emotional signs that affect how you live in the present. One typical physical sign is tiredness, which goes beyond just feeling worn out after a busy day, or a deep fatigue that persists even after getting enough rest. In addition to feeling tired all the time, you may struggle with sleeplessness at night that will keep you awake with racing thoughts and concerns. When you don't get adequate or enough sleep and your body feels drained and tired all the time, it can make you more irritable and exhausted overall.

People who have experienced traumas may be dealing with anxiety and sudden panic attacks as well. These attacks can show up out of nowhere leaving you feeling powerless and overwhelmed. Your heart might start racing, your breaths getting shorter, and your mind may start raising overwhelmed, with a sensation that this will never go away. The intensity of these moments can be so strong that they feel like a heart attack, which makes you fear even worse in those situations. Physical problems like headaches and stomach troubles often come with struggles too. Your body is trying to tell you that something isn't right and that there are things you need to address.

Sometimes feeling emotionally numb or detached is a sign too. It's like being separated by a barrier from your emotions and the people around you. The wall between you and your feelings can make it hard to truly feel happiness or sadness, or any other emotion deeply. Feeling distant from others can make you feel alone even when you're with family and have friends.

Being cautious about places or people that brings you memories is common when trying to avoid dealing with tough emotions and memories, but it can also hold you back from new experiences and growth. Being overly alert all the time is another indicator of being impacted by past events. Living in a state of vigilance can also make you feel tense and constantly wary of any dangers around you. Being alert all the time can be draining and have detrimental effects on both your mind and body.

Many people frequently use as coping mechanisms, self-destructive habits, such as substance abuse or overeating to numb their pain from traumas. These actions may offer temporary comfort but may also result in additional complications that will draw you into a challenging cycle that will be very hard to escape from. You may also encounter difficulties to build and keen relationships because of trust issues, and the fear of being abandoned can hinder your ability to open up to others, making you resort to these coping mechanisms.

- To recognize indications of trauma in your personal life consider assessing yourself using the following checklist:
- Do you have recurring nightmares or flashbacks that take you back to traumatic experiences?
- Is it a challenge for you to trust others and believe that they genuinely care about your wellbeing?

- Do you ever feel anxious about being abandoned by people you love?

Take a moment to reflect on how you react when your emotions escalate or shut down. Whether you tend to explode or become emotionally detached altogether in certain situations.

There are four types of human responses to trauma: fighting back directly against the threat (fight), fleeing from a situation (flight), becoming immobilized (freeze), or trying to calm down the imminent threat (fawn). The fight response involves confronting the perceived danger head on, either physically or verbally. You might notice yourself getting defensive in situations that trigger your sense of vulnerability, even if the threat is not immediate. When faced with danger, a threat situation, or any challenging moment, it may trigger fear or anxiety responses. We tend to react in different ways, either by instinctively running away from the source of danger or trying to distance ourselves from it, physically or emotionally. These feelings of being stuck and paralyzed and being unable to make decisions or take action produces a mental fog that clouds your thinking and hinders you from moving forward or attempting to diffuse the threat by being overly accommodating and submissive, hoping to avoid any confrontation. Sometimes you may tend to prioritize others needs over your own which can be exhausting and challenging for you in the long run.

For this reason, it's important to notice these patterns in your behavior and take the appropriate steps to address them. For example, if you feel the urge to avoid conflict or run away, simply take a moment to breathe and center yourself. Remind yourself that you are safe and focus on anchoring yourself in the moment. When you feel stuck, in a mode or in an overly compliant behavior pattern (fawning), try making gradual progress by taking small steps forward and setting clear boundaries to express your needs confidently, even if it may seem awkward in the beginning. To be able to deal with these reactions involves being self-aware and ready to face the root causes of the trauma head-on without judgment or self blame. Keep in mind that these behaviors are not shortcomings but adaptive strategies shaped by life events.

An effective route for you to effectively deal with these problems and progress towards a life of liberation and satisfaction is by understanding and facing these past problems. Remember, tracing the origins of trauma is crucial in understanding its impact.

TRACING TRAUMA TO ITS ROOTS

Exploring the origins of your pain can make you feel like solving a puzzle, piece by piece. An effective way to start this exploration is through guided journaling which is a technique that involves writing with prompts designed to encourage you to dig into your experiences and emotions. For instance, you could start by writing down your memories of fear or discomfort and reflecting on questions like "What happened during that time?" How did it impact me?" Writing can help you discover links between your feelings and past events. As you continue journaling, you might notice patterns or recurring situations in your life that are connected to unresolved issues.

Learning about your family history is another way to understand more about your roots and experiences passed down through generations. By digging into your family's past and engaging in conversations with your relatives about their life journeys and the obstacles they've overcome, can provide insights into your personal story and struggles faced by those before you. It can be truly insightful to dig into the background of your life to see how certain patterns or behaviors might have been influenced by the traumatic experiences that your parents may have gone through that shaped their parenting style, and in turn, impacted how you were raised as well.

Getting help from therapy and professionals is fundamental for understanding the roots of any trauma that might have influenced your feelings and experiences in both negative and positive ways because an experienced therapist can help you navigate your memories and emotions in a safe setting. They can guide you through different approaches like Cognitive Behavioral Therapy (CBT) or Eye Movement Desensitization and Reprocessing (EMDR) which are therapies designed to address trauma related issues. These therapeutic methods aim to help in reworking memories and reducing their impact. Therapists can also help you develop ways to manage and deal with your responses to experiences and trauma as well.

Understanding the causes of your trauma is important to help you control your reactions. Triggers are signals that revive memories of events and stir up emotional responses within us. Even a smell or a particular place can immediately recall past experiences. For example, the scent of a perfume could bring back memories of an incident involving someone dear who wore that particular perfume. Recalling events is closely tied to the way our minds handle these triggers. When something sets us off, both our minds and bodies can react strongly as if the experience is happening again, bringing back those specific memories that trigged emotional and physical responses. It is for this reason that highlighting the need to identify and understand our triggers properly is crucial to healing.

I know John, who was experiencing heightened anxiety and sudden panic attacks and, during therapy sessions, he was able to trace these episodes to a childhood trauma. His anxiety and panic attacks as an adult were rooted in the haunting memories of his abuser's distinct cologne. On another occasion, Maria felt sadness and disconnection, which she connected to her parents neglect during her upbringing. Therapy played a important role in helping her acknowledge that her emotional distance acted as a defense mechanism to be able to cope with the lack of emotional nurturing she endured in the past. These true stories I am sharing with you underscore how understanding the trauma origins, along with the assistance of therapy, can lead to you to a positive transformation.

Participating in self-exploration activities can also help you deal with trauma stemming from your experiences. You can start by creating a timeline of life events – both positive and negative – and reflect on how these events shape your beliefs, behaviors, and emotional responses. This visual representation enables you to uncover patterns and connections. Exploring questions related to your childhood memories can provide you with insights as well. You can contemplate questions, like "How did I interact with my parents?" What feelings did I have at home?" Asking these questions may bring back some memories and emotions that shed light on your experiences.

Another approach to recalling previous memories in a comforting manner is by exploring visualization exercises. Find a spot away from any distractions and close your eyes for a moment to relax your mind and emotions with a few deep breaths. Try to recall a memory from your past and focus on the details of the surroundings in that memory as well as the setting and the people present in it. Reflect on your emotions during that moment in time and imagine yourself as an observer watching that scene unfold without any judgment or criticism. This practice can help you process and reframe memories by reducing their emotional impact on you. Once you've finished imagining the scenario, pause to jot down in the journal your feelings and any thoughts that arose while you were reflecting.

These methods for identifying the origins of any wound can lead to meaningful transformations in your life. Recognizing the roots of your trauma will empower you to begin the process of addressing and healing those scars that might have hindered your progress towards healing. Embarking on this path calls for patience and self-compassionate under-standing. The insights you will acquire can prepare the way for healing and growth on a personal level.

THE IMPACT OF CHILDHOOD NEGLECT

Childhood neglect can have lasting effects on a child's devel-opment and overall well being in various ways. Emotional neglect occurs when a child's desire for love and emotional support is ignored or dismissed by by their parents or care-givers. This lack of care can lead the child to feel unappreci-ated and insignificant. It may cause them to believe that their emotions are unimportant, making it difficult for them to express themselves and form connections with others. On the hand, physical neglect involves failing to adequately provide essential necessities such as food, shelter, and medical care. Children who experience neglect often face challenges with hunger and hygiene as well as inadequate access to medical care leading to feelings of insecurity and mistrust in their surroundings. Moreover, neglect in education plays a role in failing to meet a child's educational and developmental needs—such as not enrolling them in school or providing necessary educational support and accommodations for learning disabilities. As a result of these circumstances, chil-dren may struggle academically and emotionally, impacting their self-esteem and motivation.

The lifelong effects of childhood neglect can deeply influence ones mental health into adulthood. Creating a sense of self-worth and a positive self-image can be challenging when the child's emotional needs are consistently disregarded or dismissed, leading to feelings of unworthiness for love and care; and at the same time, resulting in self doubt and need for validation from other people. Adults who have experienced neglect in their past often struggle to believe in their worth and ability to pursue their goals and dreams with confidence due to feelings of not being enough that originated from those childhood experiences. Establishing connections for them can sometimes be difficult because of the lack of an emotional foundation in the formative years that resulted in difficulties to develop trust and forging deep connections with others people. Those facing this scenario may rely significantly on others for emotional reassurance or opt to distance themselves for protection against potential hurt and disappointments.

The lasting impact of childhood neglect often make the person more susceptible to health issues. And adults who experienced neglect during their early years are constantly battling feelings of sadness and worriedness stemming from emotional scars of the past affecting their present mental well-being. This may drive some people towards substance misuse and other detrimental actions as coping mechanisms for their traumas. The persistent stress and emotional challenges they endure could also lead to lasting health issues such as blood pressure and digestive problems that will have a significant impact on their overall wellbeing.

Jane's childhood, for example, played a significant role in shaping her emotional wellbeing as she grew up in a family where her needs were often overlooked due to her parents personal struggles. Her experience led her to deal with her emotions, and later in her life, she struggled with self-confidence due to an underlying fear of rejection that stemmed from those past experiences. Jane found it challenging to form connections with others as she harbored a seated concern that people would abandon her just like her parents did. But, through therapy sessions as an adult, Jane began to recognize the impact of her upbringing on her life and she made an effort to be kind to herself and recognize her own value, which lead her to develop meaningful relationships and a boost in self-assurance over time.

However, Tom's experience with neglect in terms of wellbeing offers a contrasting perspective. Tom often faced challenges accessing basic necessities like food and medical care as he grew up in poverty. This consistent hunger and untreated ailments nurtured a sense of doubt and suspicion within him. As an adult, Tom faced trust issues towards others and chose to take control in order to establish a sense of security in his environment. But with therapy sessions, Tom was able to dig into these emotions tracing them back to his early years, and focused on developing trust and forming a network of support to recreate the feeling of security he longed for during his days.

Emily's story highlights the challenges of overcoming a lack of attention during her childhood when education was not a priority at home, so she lacked parental support at school. As a result, Emily felt uncertain and ill-prepared when confronted with life's challenges. She took control by enrolling in adult education classes and discovered a passion for learning, from both her teachers and her peers, enabling her to regain self-assurance. Since she decided to continue her education, she is now working as a teacher helping others overcome similar challenges.

Overcoming the effects of childhood neglect involves taking steps to prioritize self-compassionate and self-worth building practices as essential tasks such as speaking kindly to yourself and mindfully contemplating thoughts and emotions. It is important to challenge the beliefs we were taught in our youth and replace them with empowering thoughts while also emphasizing the significance of forming strong bonds and being part of a supportive community. Seek out people who offer encouragement and motivation as you navigate your path toward recovery. Helpful steps to take care of your wellbeing might include having friends and family members around you, participating in support groups, and seeking advice from a therapist. In addition to that, participating in activities and looking after yourself can also have a real positive impact on the process of healing. Therapy will provide a space where you can explore and address past traumas while incorporating self-care practices for overall emotional and physical wellbeing. This is crucial. Keeping a journal, practicing meditation, and engaging in exercise can aid in both the recovery journey and building resilience.

Understanding the types of neglect and how they continue to affect us allows us to face our past struggles and work towards a more fulfilling life. As you navigate your inner child and strive for personal growth and healing, remember that there are others out there going through similar experiences. You are not alone. Just keep in mind that no matter what difficulties you've faced and the marks they've left on you, there's always an opportunity for healing and self-improvement ahead of you. In the next segment of our discussion we'll explore activities and techniques to boost your path to recovery and guide you towards a life that is more emotionally free, fulfilling, and satisfying.

SETTING HEALTHY BOUNDARIES

*P*icture yourself in a city with all its hustle and bustle and all the noise and commotion surrounding you. You start to feel anxious – your heart is pounding and your palms are getting clammy. It's hard to explain the cause of this uneasiness filling you up, but it's there, it's real. This kind of feeling is something people face daily when they're carrying around traumas that are still unresolved. Those experiences can leave deep marks on our minds and bodies, whether they come from childhood trauma or from more recent events. Signs of trauma can often show up in ways that will impact our everyday routines significantly. For this reason, it's important to acknowledge and deal with them as soon as possible.

UNDERSTANDING PERSONAL BOUNDARIES

Boundaries are like personal guidelines we establish ourselves in our relationships to outline what behaviors we consider okay or not okay. The role of these boundaries is to look after our mental and physical health by safeguarding our emotional wellbeing. They can be divided into four categories: *emotional, physical, mental,* and *spiritual boundaries.* Emotional boundaries involve safeguarding our feelings. Physical boundaries is about protecting our personal space. Mental boundaries are connected to your thoughts and convictions; in other words, the way you think. These thoughts are the ones assisting in preserving your individuality and your own perspectives without submitting to external pressures for conformity. Spiritual boundaries, on the other hand, involve your faith and customs that safeguard your essence and core principles.

The significance of boundaries cannot be emphasized enough as they are crucial to avoid exhaustion by preventing you from stretching yourself too thin while striving to meet the expectations of others. The role of establishing clear boundaries is to safeguard your dignity (self-respect) and self-esteem (self-worth) by deterring others from exploiting your kindness and generosity towards others. Setting your limits will communicate your desires, needs, and expectations effectively which cultivates robust and considerate connections. When you establish boundaries effectively, you'll be more capable of handling your time and energy in what's more important, lessening persistent stress levels and improving your overall wellbeing.

Many people face challenges setting their boundaries which may impact both their personal and professional lives. For example, people-pleasers, who are people that tend to prioritize others' happiness over their own needs and desires (overall wellbeing). This tendency often originates from a fear of rejection or confrontation, making it hard for them to decline requests or establish limits. In other words, they have difficulty saying "no." If this is your case, as a result, you might feel burdened by obligations and engagements that consume your time and energy. Chronic feelings of resentment, annoyance, or frustration will develop when you consistently place the needs of others before your own, resulting in emotional fatigue and strained relationships.

To recognize your personal boundaries, you can use this self-evaluation instruction I've prepared for you:

> Think about how comfortable you're in standing up
> for what you need and want in different situations.
> Then, ask yourself: Are you faced with difficulty in
> expressing your thoughts or choices, especially when
> they don't align with those of others? Do you often
> experience feelings of guilt or anxiety when turning
> down others' requests, even though it's better
> for you?

These questions can give you some insight into how much you struggle with setting boundaries. Think about your current relationships. Do you feel like your boundaries are being disregarded or violated making you feel unseen, taken for granted, or even disrespected?

Engaging in reflective activities can also help you explore your own boundaries and recognize areas that may require reinforcement. Take a moment to reflect on situations that made you feel uneasy or upset. What particular actions or behaviors caused these emotions? How did you react to them and what was the result of your actions? By reflecting about these situations, you'll be able to identify or detect recurring patterns. Identify spots where your boundaries might be weak. This self-awareness is the first step to building better defined and more effective boundaries in your life.

I can't emphasize enough how essential it is establishing and maintaining boundaries for self-care and maintaining your wellbeing on a personal level, and how important it is acknowledging your needs and limitations while effectively communicating them to others, ensuring consistency in upholding them. This approach will help you cultivate a harmonious and satisfying life that will be devoid of persistent stress and emotional disruption commonly associated with boundary challenges. Remember that his process will require practice, lots of patience, and self-compassion as you dig deeper into identifying and comprehending those personal boundaries.

TECHNIQUES FOR SETTING BOUNDARIES

Establishing boundaries involves communicating by expressing your feelings and needs tactfully but acknowledging others' perspectives as well. An important strategy is using "I" statements instead of accusatory language such as "You never pay attention to me." Instead, you can say "I feel disregarded when I'm interrupted." This approach shifts the focus from blaming the other person to sharing your experience (how YOU feel), which will help the other person grasp your viewpoint without feeling defensive. Using straightforward language is essential too. State your needs or expectations directly and precisely. Try to be more specific when asking for help than making vague requests like "I wish you would help me more?" Be direct and specific about what you want or need by saying, for example, "Please remember to empty the trash on Wednesday." Practicing active listening during conversations is equally important when setting boundaries – take the time to understand the other person's viewpoint and respond thoughtfully by acknowledging their emotions and finding compromises that cater to everyone's requirements (finding a middle ground).

Engaging in role playing scenarios also serves as a method to hone your boundary setting skills within a secure setting. Let's do an exercise. Picture a situation where you're faced with a controlling family member who tends to make decisions for you (we all have one of those). During this role play exercise, you can practice articulating saying phrases like:

"Thank you for your concern; however I must make this decision myself."

This practice will let you to assert your boundaries without the stress of an actual confrontation. Alternatively, you could simulate a scenario involving a colleague who frequently requests that you cover his/her shifts. Saying "I see that you need my help; however, at this moment, I am unable to work additional shifts" is a useful phrase you can practice in similar scenarios where it will be necessary to assert limits firmly but respectfully. Consider this other scenario with a friend who crosses boundaries by borrowing your possessions without seeking permission. Practicing communication like saying: "I feel uncomfortable when my belongings are borrowed without asking me first, could you please ask for permission the next time?" can be beneficial in such instances. Engaging in role-playing scenarios like these can really build your confidence while strengthening your ability to establish boundaries with clarity and effectiveness.

Using tools like diagrams and worksheets can also be helpful in setting boundaries. For instance, a worksheet designed for setting boundaries can guide you through the steps of identifying, recognizing and expressing your limits or boundaries clearly. For example, write down the instances or situations when you felt that your boundaries were often violated, and also write down phrases you could use to address them. Creating these tangible visual representations of your personal space and emotional boundaries can help you understand and communicate your boundaries more effectively. These exercises are extremely important, so, put them into practice.

Keep in mind that consistency is key when it comes to upholding boundaries; for this reason, it is important to enforce those boundaries to send the message that they are *non-negotiable* and must be respected. One technique to remain firm is to repeat your boundaries, calmly and clearly, when someone tries to test your limits. For example, to remind your colleague that you're unable to take on extra work, gently and with a firm tone, you can remind them: "I've already mentioned that I'm unable to handle additional work at the moment." Always acknowledge the other person's feelings while remaining firm to your decision. Saying, for example: "I see that you're not happy about it; however, my choice remains the same." Continuously reassessing and refining your boundaries is essential to ensure they continue to benefit you. Make adjustments as needed and keep others informed about any modifications, as this will keep harmonious and respectful connections.

You will probably experience resistance from others when you establish boundaries. They may resist and test your limits, and even try to manipulate you with guilt. I remember the times when my brother needed me to do something for him and I would say I couldn't. He started telling me the many ways I would benefit from saying yes to what he was asking me to do. I always ended up doing what he was asking, but in doing that I resented him and myself because I was doing something I didn't want to do or was unable to do.

After many years of this dynamic, I made the decision that I wouldn't give up no matter the many reasons he had come up with to make me feel guilty in order to convince me to do his will. So, I told him how I felt about it. He obviously denied he was trying to manipulate me because from his point of view that wasn't his intention, but that's the way he was coming across. From them on, every time I couldn't do what he was asking, I would say no and and I stood firm in my decision. That felt like a liberation to me!

For this reason, it is vital to remain firm and consistent in your decisions. Establishing limits is not a matter of a single occurrence but a continuous process that will demand self-awareness and clear communication skills while prioritizing your own needs in order to foster healthier and more satis-fying relationships.

PRACTICING BOUNDARY SETTING IN DAILY LIFE

To incorporate boundary-setting routines, begin your mornings with affirmations that reinforce those boundaries. Simple phrases such as "It's okay to say no" or "My needs are important" can set a positive tone for the rest of your day.

Using a planner to plan out your time ensures you put self-care first and maintain your boundaries. Set aside blocks of time for activities that will help you recharge, such as going out for a walk, reading a good book, or even just relaxing without any distractions. When you incorporate these activities into your schedule, you are sending a strong message to yourself and others that your wellbeing and time are valuable priorities. This habit serves as a safeguard, against overcommitment and burnout.

When establishing your boundaries, must use different strategies according to the situation at hand. For example, whenever you feel swamped at work, communicate your limitations to your manager to improve balance and productivity while meeting deadlines and commitments. You can say something like this: "I can take on this new project, but I'lll need to extend the deadline from my current tasks." When at home, establishing your boundaries poses its unique set of challenges too — particularly when dealing with relatives unexpected visits without prior notice. Kindly tell them that you enjoy their company but need them to let you know before dropping by so that you can organize your schedule accordingly. You can say, for example: "I love spending time with you but I need heads-up before visiting so that I can plan my schedule accordingly." This will help create a respectful dynamic between the two.

Social boundaries also play an important role in safeguarding your mental wellbeing by setting limitations to your interactions on social media platforms. Choose designated times to check your social media accounts and make sure to adhere to those specific times. If you're often tagged or invited by friends, let them know your preferences. This kind of communication aids in setting expectations clearly and preserving your sense of comfort.

Make sure to prioritize these practices like you would any other significant commitment. Listen to your body and mind, which will cue you for when it's time to take a break. If you're feeling swamped or anxious give yourself permission to pause to recharge. This could involve taking a day off to focus on your wellbeing or indulging in activities that bring you joy. Practicing self-care through these techniques and engaging in activities is like any other exercise and hobbies that bring happiness.

When you want to communicate your boundaries, try using scripts for various situations as a guide. For example, if you have to turn down an invitation, firmly say: "Thank you for the invite but I've got other plans that day." This kind of response is considerate yet assertive without room for negotiation. Similarly, when dealing with a breach of boundaries, address it directly saying: "It made me uncomfortable when you used my things without asking." This dialogue tackles the problem without making it worse by causing a conflictive situation.

It may seem obvious, but those with emotional baggage may struggle to be assertive and express their desires. Keep in mind that setting boundaries is a way of showing self-value and contributes to maintaining positive connections and overall health.

MAINTAINING BOUNDARIES OVER TIME

Keeping boundaries intact over time can pose a challenge as you navigate through different situations in your life. Dealing with those who are constantly pushing your limits – the boundary pushers – can be quite a task to handle on a regular basis as they tend to make you feel guilty or question your boundaries by arguing against them. Another big obstacle is overcoming the feelings of guilt and fear of rejection that often come along with setting boundaries. It's natural to seek approval and want to be accepted by others; however, this desire can sometimes lead you to compromise your boundaries in order to please them. It's also important to address the issue of fatigue that may arise over time as you maintain these boundaries. Setting boundaries can be quite draining when faced with constant resistance and pushback from others. Feeling tired can make it challenging to maintain those boundaries effectively and might undo all your hard work in an instant if your are not careful.

Evaluate your boundaries on a regular basis to make sure they are still beneficial to you. If you discover that certain boundaries are no longer relevant or helpful, don't hesitate to adapt and make changes, or eliminate them altogether. Seeking guidance from trusted people can also help strengthen these boundaries. Share your boundary-setting experiences with loved ones and a therapist, if needed. They can support, advise, and keep you accountable to maintain your boundaries.

Setting and respecting boundaries has many benefits, including improved wellbeing, increased ability to handle life's challenges, and healthier relationships based on mutual respect and understanding. These benefits can lead to more fulfilling interactions and connections with others. Moreover, setting limits helps in enhancing your strength and self-respect. You will be able to establish boundaries and stick to them if you remain vigilant and proactive. The long-term advantages will be evident: improved emotional wellbeing, respectful interactions with others, and a stronger feeling of empowerment and self-esteem.

In the next section, we'll discuss handling emotional triggers, moving you closer to emotional wellness and resilience.

MANAGING EMOTIONAL TRIGGERS

*Y*ou are at a family event and someone mentions a name that triggers your anxiety, making your heart race and palms sweat. Even though the reaction may seem exaggerated for the moment's context, it serves as a strong reminder of how past encounters can impact your present emotional wellbeing. This scenario showcases a trigger at play – instinctive reactions from triggers that evoke recollections of previous traumas or unresolved battles. These stimuli have the potential to manifest in various ways, such as fragrances in the air, distinct sounds or visuals that can unexpectedly evoke intense emotional responses. Emotional triggers are like unexpected treasures waiting to be discovered. They remain inactive until a particular stimulus awakens them and unleashes a flood of sentiments that may be overpowering at times. For example: A familiar fragrance of a cologne can swiftly whisk you back to an unsettling episode associated with the person who wore it. Likewise, the sound of approaching footsteps from behind might evoke sensations of unease and alarm if you has faced an encounter involving assault. Being in a room of people can unexpectedly stir up memories of feeling confined or powerless from past encounters.

Our emotional reactions are heavily influenced by these early memories. An adult that has been constantly criticized as a child, will probably develop feelings of intense inadequacy and feeling ashamed whenever he/she receives from a colleague a simple remark about his/her work's performance. Lets explore some examples to illustrate this scenario. Consider Sarah's childhood in a home filled with arguments and shouting. As a grown up, this loud sound of voices during a simple argument can trigger in her anxiousness and fear each time it happens. Jake, for example, experienced childhood neglect, which made him feel abandoned and angry whenever he smells alcohol because it reminded him of his father's breath.

A self-assessment can help you identify your own triggers. Begin by reflecting on your recent emotional reactions by asking yourself, "When did I last feel an intense emotional response?" and "What was happening at that particular moment?" This reflection can help you pinpoint situations or things that provoked (triggered) your emotions. One practical exercise is to make a list of the physical and emotional reactions that you have when triggered. Include in your list signs like feelings of a raised heart bit, an accelerated breathing, or even having sweaty palms, and write down how these reactions make you feel. Whether anxious or angry, etc. You will be aware of your triggers by referring to this list because you'll discover how these triggers manifest physically and emotionally.

You need to keep track of what triggers you over time so you can manage them effectively. A good idea would be to maintain a "trigger diary." Whenever you feel an strong emotional response coming on, take a moment to write down the specifics. Include the date and time of the trigger event along with where you were and what triggered it, and describe how you felt emotionally and physically in that moment. By doing this, you might start noticing patterns that could help pinpoint your specific triggers and understand when they are most likely to happen. Consider also using apps or journals to keep track of your reactions in a structured manner. You'll find that many mental health apps include tools for logging and reviewing responses to help you identify recurring patterns. Check out apps like:

1. EMoodTracker - https://emoodtracker.com/
2. Mind Tracker available via Google Play
3. Mood Notes - Mood Tracker available from Apple store
4. Search the web for 'mood trackers' for additional apps

The next step to analyze these patterns is understanding your triggers so that you can cope with them and manage them better to promote inner child healing. Identify themes or specific situations that provoke strong responses in you. For example, you might observe that some social settings tend to trigger feelings of anxiety or even certain times of the year like holidays could also trigger feelings of grief or sadness.

Handling triggers plays a vital role in the process of nurturing your inner child's healing journey. Recognizing the cues that stir up your emotions and linking them to hurts empowers you to proactively tackle and mend those wounds. This process demands patience and self-awareness. Just remember that every step you take propels you towards a future enriched with emotional liberation, strength, and ultimately freedom.

GROUNDING TECHNIQUES FOR EMOTIONAL STABILITY

Grounding techniques can be really helpful for bringing your attention to the present moment whenever you're feeling overwhelmed by emotional triggers from past situations. These are techniques that involve your senses to help you connect with what's happening in front of you. This practice can do wonders for reducing anxiety and promoting a sense of peace. It's like having a shield ready to protect you from negative emotions and regain control. Giving you the chance to take a breath and get back in charge whenever those triggers pop up. These techniques are breathing techniques that act as a way to clear your mind and help you shift your focus away from the negative, from whatever is bothering you.

A very effective technique for grounding is the 5-2-3-2-1 coping method where you engage your senses to keep yourself in the present moment. You would start by identifying 5 things you can see around you. Pause for a moment to really notice the details around you — like colors, shapes, and textures. Next, notice 4 things near you that you can touch. This time, focus on the sensations beneath your fingertips, this could be the smooth surface of a table or fabric, etc. Now, focus on 3 things you can hear, concentrating on the sounds in your immediate surroundings. It could be the gentle whir of an air conditioner or the faint sound of traffic in the distance. Next, identify 2 unique scents around you. Consider keeping a small item with a delightful fragrance handy in case your current setting lacks any particular smell. Lastly, pinpoint 1 thing you can taste and notice the flavor. You can take a sip of a drink or chew some gum as part of this exercise. The purpose of all this is to help shift your focus from thoughts and bring you back to the current moment.

Another effective exercise is a deep breathing exercise which is another grounding method to combat anxiety by deep breathing during moments of stress when shallow breathing and panic intensify due to the change in breathing patterns. It will help calm your nervous system. To practice this breathing technique, follow these steps:

1. Find a comfortable seating position.
2. Place one hand over your chest while the other hand is gently positioned over your abdomen.
3. Inhale slowly through your nose as you allow your stomach to expand with each breath that fills your lungs.

4. Hold your breath for a count of four, then exhale through your mouth noticing the gentle fall of your abdomen.
5. Repeat this technique several times while focusing on your breathing, its rhythm pattern.

This exercise will ease your stress quickly bringing a sense of calmness to you, reducing the any anxiety.

Progressive muscle relaxation is a method or technique that involves slowly tensing and relaxing different muscle groups in your body deliberately.

1. Find a spot to sit or lie down comfortably before starting the exercise. Start with your toes.
2. Curl your toes tightly for a moment before releasing the grip and experiencing the feeling of relaxation as you release the tension.
3. Progress through your body by concentrating on each group of muscles — starting from your calves and moving upwards to your thighs abdomen, chest, arms, and finally, the face.

Practicing this activity aids in easing strain that often results with emotional pressure and encourages a feeling of tranquility and ease (relaxation).

Consistent practice plays an important role in maximizing the effectiveness of these grounding methods. Try to make them a regular part of your daily schedule so that you become more comfortable with them over time and become easier.

Start your mornings with a brief session of deep breathing or try out the 5-4-3-2-1 technique during your lunch hour. The more you practice these techniques, the faster they'll become second nature when you need them the most. Also integrate the grounding practices into your daily routine. These methods will create a routine until it becomes a habit that will allow for easier use of the techniques when you are facing any emotional triggers.

Let's take Emma's experience, for example. She was dealing with severe anxiety when speaking in public settings. She adopted the 5–4–3–2–1 sensory strategy to ease her nerves and calm down before a presentation on stage. By focusing on her environment, she successfully redirected her focus away from her anxiety and gave her speech with confidence. Another example is James, who engaged in deep breathing exercises before to important meetings. By dedicating a few moments to center himself, he discovered that he could approach discussions with a calm and clear mind, decreasing his stress levels. These true life examples demonstrate how these grounding methods can be smoothly incorporated into any scenario providing you immediate relief and efficient emotional comfort during moments of distress.

MINDFULNESS PRACTICES FOR TRIGGER MANAGEMENT

Mindfulness means staying in the present moment and being aware without any judgment involved. It is about focusing your attention on your thoughts and feelings as they happen.

This approach can be really helpful for handling triggers because it allows you to see how you react without getting carried away by those reactions. By practicing mindfulness, you give yourself space to choose how to respond rather than reacting automatically. The advantages of using mindfulness to manage emotions are widely recognized and used today because it has the potential to lessen feelings of worriedness and tension while enhancing your wellbeing by keeping you connected to the present moment.

Engaging in mindfulness techniques can be a wonderful addition to your everyday routine because it's easy to incorporate it at any time by simply focusing on your breath and observing every inhalation and exhalation. Find a spot to sit down, close your eyes, and gently take a deep breath in through your nostrils, hold your breath for a moment, and then exhale slowly through your mouth. Notice how your chest expands as you fill your lungs with air. As you breathe, focus on the sensation of the air flowing in and out of your body. When your thoughts stray off track during meditation, gently guide them back to your breathing rhythm to focus and calm your mind.

Another beneficial mindfulness technique is the *body meditation* or *body scan* where you focus your attention on various body parts to notice any sensation, tension, or discomfort you may feel. Find a spot to lie down with your eyes closed as you begin and focus your attention to your toes first acknowledging any warmth, coolness, or pressure that you may sense. Now, shift your focus upwards, gradually starting from your feet and moving through your ankles and calves, all the way up to your head; taking time to notice each body part without any judgement. This exercise will be beneficial to increase your body awareness and releasing any tension that might be linked to your emotional stress.

Mindful walking is a practice that involves focusing on the sensations in your feet and legs while walking to be aware of muscle tension and the earth beneath your feet. This practice can be done anywhere, from walks in a park to daily walks to work. This helps you stay present and connected to your body, while reducing stress and managing emotional triggers.

Let's start a mindfulness practice by concentrating on our breath. First, find a spot where you can have some peace and quiet without any interruptions around you. To begin this exercise, sit down in a comfortable position and close your eyes.

1. Take a slow breath in through your nose and pay close attention to how your lungs expand.
2. Hold your breath for a count of four before releasing it out through your mouth.
3. While you are breathing in this way, focus on how the air feels as it flows in and out of your body.
4. If you notice your thoughts starting to wander off track, guide them back gently, and continue focusing on your breath.
5. Spend five to ten minutes practicing this exercise while focusing on relaxing with each breath.

Now, let's try the body scan medication exercise. Just get cozy lying down and close your eyes and take a few deep breaths for a bit of relaxation before starting.

1. Take a moment to focus on your toes and feel any sensations there before moving up slowly through each part of your body.
2. Spend some time in each area as you go along. No need for judgment as you observe any tension or discomfort that pops up along the way.
3. If you happen to notice any tense spots, ease them by picturing your breath flowing there and helping them relax.
4. Repeat these steps until you've scanned all your body thoroughly.
5. Finally, wrap up with a couple of deep breaths to experience a calm sensation connected to your body.

Incorporating similar mindfulness exercises into your routine doesn't demand a lot of time or energy investment at all! You can practice *mindful eating* for example. When you eat, pay close attention to the flavors, consistency and scents of your food. Take your time to chew and savor your food while being mindful of the sensations in your mouth and the process of swallowing. This approach not only enriches your dining experience but also assists you in being fully engaged and present during meals.

You can also practice mindfulness while you are doing your daily chores, like doing the dishes or folding laundry. Pay attention to what you're doing, seeing, smelling, and sounds around you at that moment. If your mind wanders off elsewhere, bring them back to present moment.

Don't forget to schedule in some moments for mindfulness throughout your day! You can set alarms on your phone or a timer to remind you at times to take a break and practice mindfulness exercises. Take short breaks to strengthen mindfulness and stay present, improving your ability to handle emotions.

BUILDING EMOTIONAL RESILIENCE

Emotional resilience refers to the capacity to adjust and recuperate from pressure of difficult situations or trauma. It's like a mental muscle that gets stronger with time enabling you to recover fast and efficiently from emotional obstacles. This strength is vital to managing triggers as it will provide you with the skills and perspective needed to manage disruptions without feeling overwhelmed and long-term emotional well-being reaps significant rewards from this resilience as it nurtures a feeling of steadiness and contentment, even amidst life's unavoidable trials.

To cultivate resilience, it is essential to adopt an attitude from the outset that recognizes the challenges while emphasizing the opportunities for personal development they offer. Having a positive mindset entails acknowledging your own abilities and leveraging them to overcome obstacles. It's also about reframing your viewpoint from "Why's this happening to me?" to "What lessons can I learn from this experience?"

This change in perspective will greatly impact how you handle and cope with emotional stressors.

Practicing self-kindness is also another method for developing resilience during challenging situations. It's about treating yourself with the same care and empathy as you would treat a friend. When you come across a situation or setback, instead of being critical about yourself, recognize your emotions and reassure yourself that it's normal to face difficulties. Self-compassion helps in nurturing inner dialogue, which is important for emotional resilience because it enables you to recover from struggles faster and promotes a better self-understanding and connection with yourself.

Strengthening social bonds is also important for resilience to have a support system that can offer you both emotional and practical help during tough times. Establishing and nurturing relationships with empathetic individuals can also give you a feeling of belonging and safety. These type of connections will serve as a shield against stress and make you feel less alone when facing emotional challenges. Getting involved in community events or becoming part of support groups will further strengthen your circle and offer extra support.

Establish a support system is vital for enhancing resilience in challenging times. Participate in activities like club memberships or group hobbies to foster connections with others. Engaging in a variety of activities aids in building new relationships and fortifying existing ones to create a reliable support network. Sharing your stories and struggles with others, not only offers fresh viewpoints but also emotional comfort that reinforces your resilience.

You should try adding practical exercises into your daily schedule to boost your emotional strength and endurance and withstand challenges life throws your way. You will also benefit form keeping a gratitude journal where you cam jot down the things you appreciate each day. This simple exercise will help shift your attention from negativity to positivity, fostering a more positive outcome. So take time to acknowledge the good in your life as it promote resilience by reinforcing feelings of appreciation and satisfaction.

Besides the gratitude journal, another effective method to strengthen resilience is engaging in self-talk exercises, just like reframing your viewpoint we discussed earlier. With self-talk, you recognize negative thoughts and substitute them with uplifting thoughts. For example, if you notice yourself thinking "This is much for me to handle " switch it up with "I have the ability and strength to handle this." Positive self-talk has the power to shift your perspective and simplify dealing with stress and emotional triggers.

Let me share Lisa's story. She went through a time when she lost her job, but instead of giving up, she chose to concentrate on things she could control. She started writing a gratitude journal every day to remind herself of the things in her life she was thankful for. She also joined a group for job seekers where she found comfort and useful tips. Thanks to her attitude and the encouragement from her new friends, Lisa not only landed a new job but also regained her self-confidence, resilience, and ability to bounce back from any setback.

Another example is Mark's journey. He struggled with anxiety and emotional triggers linked to past traumatic experiences. He started incorporating self-kindness and positive self-talk into his routine to reassure himself that feeling anxious was normal and that he had the capacity to handle it effectively. Moreover, Mark strengthened his social connections by engaging with friends and becoming a part of a mindfulness community. These approaches helped him in developing emotional strength (resilience) and enabled him to handle triggers constructively easier.

If you work and focus on strengthening your emotional mindset and resilience skills, you will be able to handle life's challenges effectively and realize that managing triggers and sustaining emotional wellbeing becomes smoother.

TRANSFORMING NEGATIVE SELF-TALK

*T*hink about you, standing in front of a mirror preparing for an event and, as you prepare your outfit, a little voice in you whispers doubts like: " You might not be good enough. You could end up embarrassing yourself." This critical inner voice tends to shake your confidence and self-esteem as it keeps on nitpicking and second guesses your every move like a critical observer highlighting all your imperfections and your missteps.

Your inner critic is the voice in your head that judges and puts you down. Its origin is normally from your childhood experiences, and too often, from parents or siblings. All those negative things you heard while growing up that are now part of how you talk to yourself as they have been internalized. The inner critic often involves being overly critical of oneself and setting unrealistic standards while struggling to recognize accomplishments effectively. It tends to magnify your mistakes and undermine your achievements, making it difficult to feel confident and competent.

The inner critic has an impact on both self-esteem and mental well-being that shouldn't be underestimated. Self-judging yourself constantly will diminish your self-worth and confidence over time. When you are consistently criticizing yourself, you eventually internalize those thoughts and start believing in them. This negative self-perception will trigger an increase level of anxiety and depression since the inner voice reinforces feelings of inadequacy and despair. This thought pattern forms a vicious cycle that's challenging to break. Moreover this inner critic acts as a barrier to development and accomplishments. It's common to feel held back by the fear of failure which can stop you from taking risks or pursuing your goals successfully. Your inner critic's voice can be very persuasive to convince your to avoid challenges and opportunities that could otherwise help you reach your full potential.

To assist you in recognizing your inner critic's voice, you can start with a self-assessment tool that includes reflective questions aimed at helping you identify common self-critical thoughts. For example, ask yourself questions like "Do I tend to compare myself to others?" or "Do I downplay my accomplishments as mere luck or unwarranted?" Such questions can aid you pinpoint the impact of the critic on your thought process; in other words, how it influences your thinking. Additionally, keeping checklist outlining behaviors of the inner critic may prove beneficial. Search for recurring behaviors such as pursuing perfectionism, procrastination, or anxiety. Behaviors like these are usually the result of your inner critic setting unrealistic standards and being afraid of failure. Journaling prompts can help dig into the origins of your inner critic. A good exercise is to write about your memories of feeling criticized or judged and reflect on who those voices belonged to and how they affected you. This activity can reveal the origins of your critic and offer insights into how it developed so that you can manage it.

To recognize that voice within you takes mindfulness and self-awareness into account. Mindfulness exercises can assist you in observing your self-talk as it unfolds naturally. Try to focus on your thoughts without passing judgment on them, and when a self critical idea surfaces in your mind, simply acknowledge it without getting caught up in it. Just acknowledge it by telling to yourself: "That must be my inner critic speaking." Then, allow it to fade away. Keeping a journal of your thoughts can enhance your awareness of your inner critic. Make a list of self-criticism's thoughts as they arise and include the circumstances and how you feel emotionally at that moment. This method can help you uncover patterns and triggers that will help you understand when and why your critic shows up. Recognizing the factors that prompt self-criticism is key to dealing with it. Typical triggers could be circumstances or individuals that cause you stress. For instance, you might observe that your inner critic speaks up before a significant event or during a stressful moment, but if you recognized the triggers, it will help you handle them proactively rather than reactively.

One way to combat the inner critic is by acknowledging its actions and using various strategies to overcome it. For example, you can challenge your inner critic by showing yourself the same kindness you would show a friend. If you find yourself thinking "I am a failure," try reframing it as " I have made a mistake. I am learning and evolving." Additionally, recognizing imperfections as a part of being human, can help diminish the power of the inner critic. Remember that everyone makes mistakes and that these errors do not determine your value. Fostering a sense of gratitude will help you redirect your attention from what you may see as shortcomings to your strengths and accomplishments. Recognizing the things you appreciate each day will lead to an optimistic and well rounded perspective. And, getting support from therapists or counselors can provide you with techniques and resources for handling your self-talk as their expert advice will support you in cultivating a positive inner dialogue and strengthening your ability to combat self-criticism.

DEVELOPING POSITIVE AFFIRMATIONS

Using statements to reshape your thinking and challenge negative self-talk (positive affirmations) is a powerful method with the potential to rewire your mind in a positive way. With practice of affirmations comes a training effect of reprogramming your brain to embrace more optimistic thought patterns instead of dwelling in negativity. The effectiveness of affirmations stems from their capacity to forge neural connections within your brain's complex network. As you consistently repeat positive messages to yourself, you are reinforcing or strengthening these neural pathways — leading your mind towards a default inclination for positivity instead of negativity. Replacing your thoughts with positive affirmations like "I am strong and capable" instead of "I am weak and useless" will gradually change your mindset for the better and contribute to a more positive self-perception as well. As a result, you'll enhance your mental health or well-being over time.

There are several essential steps to follow diligently in order to craft these affirmations. Begin by discerning and recognizing when negative self-talk plagues your mind and keeps resurfacing in your consciousness every day. After pinpointing these recurring patterns of negativity and self doubt within yourself, the next step is to transform those negative thoughts into uplifting ones, into empowering statements. For example, if you often think "I'll never be successful," reframe your thought with "I have the necessary skills and determination to achieve my goals." Also, use present tense. Say "I am happy and content" instead of saying "I will be happy." Practicing this emotional language with affirmations in present tense, will bring more power to your affirmations and help your mind internalize them; which in turn, will make this practice effective.

Affirmations that work well cover a range of areas in your life, addressing different aspects of your self-perception (how you see yourself) and your aspirations in life. To boost your self-worth you can say "I am valued, I am enough just as I am." These statements will emphasize your self-worth regardless of external approval. For building resilience and inner strength, you could say: "I have the strength to tackle any challenge that comes my way." This affirmation will empower you to face any adversity. When it comes to self-love and acceptance, you can repeat affirmations such as "I'm worthy of love and kindness," which will remind you to be kind and compassionate to yourself. You can come up with your own affirmations tailored to your needs and situations for a more personalized and impactful experience.

Start your mornings with a routine of affirmations to set a tone for the day. Take a few moments every morning to repeat these affirmations either loud or silently to yourself. This simple practice can help you cultivate a mindset throughout the day. Consider jotting down your affirmations on notes and placing them in various spots around your living space. Stick them on places like the mirror in your bathroom or, on the fridge and desk to keep them visible and encourage thinking throughout the day. These visual reminders will help you keep your affirmations at the fore-front of your mind.

Apps and recordings can aid in improving your mindset and motivation as well. They include features for reminders, progress tracking, and positive affirmations to support you along the way. These resources will reinforce your affirma-tions' routine. Record yourself reciting these statements and listen to them at different times throughout the day. Hearing your own voice can have a powerful impact, strengthening the message on a personal level.

Talk to yourself standing in front of the mirror and saying: "Good things are meant for me; I deserve them." While you're brushing your teeth and looking at your reflection in the mirror, repeat to yourself: "I am confident and capable." Setup a reminder from your affirmation app prompting you to pause and declare "I am successful and worthy." Engaging in these simple, but regular activities can influence your mindset and well-being.

Using affirmations isn't a fix for everything but they can be very effective in handling emotions and turning around negative self-talk habits. Make it a habit to incorporate them into your routine to alter your perspective and develop a more optimistic self-perception. This transformation process demands dedication and time, but the benefits outweigh the challenges. Remember that you hold the capability to reshape your thoughts and consequently transform your own life.

SELF-COMPASSION PRACTICES

You should treat yourself with the same compassion and understanding as you treat a close friend in need. Recognizing that everyone goes through challenges and makes mistakes is important to maintain mental health. Self-kindness involves being kind with yourself without being overly critical. Understanding that suffering and feelings of inadequacy are common human experiences will help you feel connected rather than isolated from others. Practicing mindfulness means acknowledging your pain without getting caught up in it or trying to ignore it.

Practicing self-compassion can have an impact on your mental and emotional health by reducing anxiety and depression levels through breaking the cycle of self-criticism and negative inner dialogue. When you show yourself compassion and understanding, you cultivate a nurturing atmosphere that promotes emotional balance. This leads to resilience making it easier for you to recover from setbacks. Moreover, people who engage in self-kindness practices often express levels of satisfaction with life in general. People often find that they enjoy connections with others when they embrace self-kindness and understanding of their imperfections, all while maintaining a positive attitude towards life. Practicing self-compassion involves recognizing your shortcomings and missteps without letting them overwhelm you – ultimately leading to a harmonious and satisfying lifestyle.

There are practical activities you can integrate into your routine to nurture self-compassion in your life. One such impactful technique is "loving-kindness meditation" which focuses on sending caring and affectionate thoughts to both yourself and those around you. Find a spot to sit and close your eyes as you begin the practice. Start by repeating phrases such as "May I be happy," "May I be healthy," and "May I be safe." Extend these sentiments to others in your life, including those who may pose challenges for you. This meditation practice helps cultivate feelings of unity and empathy, towards both yourself and others.

Whenever you feel stressed out, take a moment to practice the tips discussed earlier in this chapter. Take a break to recognize your struggle, and tell yourself: "This is a temporary moment of hardship. Difficulties are just part of life." Then, gently place your hands on your heart and offer yourself some comforting words and encouragement by saying "May I be kind to myself in this needing moment." As simple as it sounds, this exercise will bring comfort and help you deal with challenging emotions smoothly.

It can be helpful to try writing a letter to yourself as though you were a friend during times of distress or difficulty in your life. For example, if you feel down because you made a mistake at work, you might write something like this: "It's okay to feel disappointed; mistakes happen to everyone at some point or another. I am doing the best I can, and that's what's important." Remember that your effort and dedication are what truly matter in the end, and this activity could change how you see things and support you in developing an inner conversation.

Lets consider the case of Elena for a moment – she struggled with self-criticism following a relationship that didn't work out well for her. She blamed herself of the failure and doubted if she deserved love at all. But, with the help of therapy, she started engaging in activities that foster self-compassion, like "loving kindness meditation" and "self-compassion breaks." As time went by, Elena observed a decrease in her anxiety levels and discovered a sense of calm within herself (inner peace). She started seeing herself from a forgiving perspective, a shift that improved her mental wellness and allowed her to build healthier relationships and connections with others.

Now, let me share Michael's story. He experienced burnout from his demanding job because he was overly self-critical and was constantly striving for more success. Michael began writing letters to himself as though from a caring friend to cope with this pressure and find the much needed peace. These heartfelt letters helped him appreciate his efforts and realize the importance of taking time for himself. This approach led Michael to develop a work life balance decreasing his stress levels and boosting his overall job satisfaction.

Keep in mind that incorporating self-compassion into your routine requires regular effort and a readiness to treat yourself kindly. These activities are designed to assist you in establishing a base of empathy and insight that will change how you interact with yourself. You'll cultivate a more encouraging and caring inner atmosphere that will enhance your emotional state substantially, enabling you handle life's challenges successfully.

REWRITING YOUR INNER NARRATIVE

Your inner narrative is what you tell yourself every day. That monologue that molds how you see yourself and how you act in the world around you. Your inner narrative shapes your identity and ambitions. Affects everything from how sure of yourself you are to how you interact with people. A pessimistic inner narrative can harm your self-worth and lead you to behaviors that will hold you back. When you keep convincing yourself that you lack ability or that you'll not succeed, those beliefs will get deeply rooted in your mind and start influencing how you behave and the choices you make.

Switching your mindset about your inner narrative plays a key role in personal development and satisfaction in life. Turning yourself into an advocate for a positive self-perception will help you break away from restrictive beliefs that may hinder your progress. When you have faith in your abilities, you become prone to venture out of your comfort zone, take risks and seize chances that pave the way for accomplishments. It is because of this that transforming the way you talk to yourself, your inner narrative, can also aid in combatting self-defeating behaviors where you unconsciously obstruct your own path to achieve your goals and aspirations. You are able to boost your overall happiness and help yourself in achieving your maximum capabilities just by fostering a positive self-perception or self-image..

If you really want to transform your inner narrative, you can start by examining and confronting your beliefs at the core of your inner thoughts to kick off the process of reshaping or transforming your mindset from within. Typically rooted in childhood experiences are these beliefs about oneself that may revolve around notions such as "I am unworthy of love" or "I will never succeed." Dedicate some moments to ponder over these convictions and challenge their truthfulness. Pose inquiries, like "Whats the origin of this belief?" Does it stand upon evidence or mere suppositions?" Writing down your thoughts may assist in clarifying and questioning these convictions about yourself. After pinpointing your foundational beliefs, it's now the time to craft a new narrative about yourself, a fresh and uplifting personal story about yourself. This updated story should reflect your capabilities, achievements and potential, avoiding dwelling on your restrictions, but rather showcasing your talents and victories. For example, substitute "I'm constantly making mistakes" with " I gain knowledge and evolve from each situation." Make sure to store this story in a spot that allows you to revisit it frequently to remind yourself of its uplifting message.

Visualization techniques are another way to bring to life your new inner narrative. Just take a moment to close your eyes and picture yourself experiencing this positive story about yourself. See yourself reaching your goals while interacting with others positively and overcoming obstacles with resilience. Imagine these scenarios as if they were happening now. This mental visualization can help you make the new storyline seem tangible to you, and within reach. Visualization serves as a bridge between how you view or perceive yourself and the positive self-image you aspire to cultivate for your self. We'll talk more about visualization techniques in Chapter 7.

Practicing positive inner narrative requires continuous dedication (effort) and introspection (self-reflection). Frequent journaling can help you in staying in touch with your new narrative, your mindset. When journaling, take time to reflect on your experiences and observe how this new narrative is influencing the way you think and act. Practice journaling whenever you face challenges along the way to process your emotions and strengthen your beliefs. Also, engaging in affirmations and expressing gratitude play a role in reinforcing your inner narrative. Star your mornings by reciting uplifting affirmations that resonate with your new narrative (your self story) and always remember to appreciate your strengths and accomplishments— even the little ones! Doing this will help you shift your mindset (focus) from negativity to positivity, and strengthening your new narrative.

Building connections with people who uplift and have faith in you is important for reinforcing a positive self-perception. For this reason, it's you should surround yourself with people who inspire and support you because their encouragement plays the important role of helping you internalize your new inner narrative. Participate in activities and environments that nurture your personal development and overall well-ness. Whether its becoming part of a welcoming community or indulging in hobbies that bring happiness, or setting up a positive workspace. These external factors greatly influence how you view yourself.

In the following chapter, we'll discover the power of vulnera-bility and how embracing it could cultivate stronger bonds and personal development growth within ourselves. Remember that, by reshaping your inner narrative, you are laying the foundation for a happier and more fulfilling life. This change is not merely an single occurrence but rather an ongoing process that demands patiences with consistent effort and self-compassion. Continue nurturing your new inner narrative and soon enough you'll witness significant transformations in your confidence levels and overall wellbeing.

OVERCOMING FEAR OF VULNERABILITY

*I*magine being at a gathering with friends and acquaintances where you are laughing and engaging in conversations while still feeling a hint of hesitation deep within that keeps you from fully revealing your authentic self to others. I'have felt that sometimes in my life too. Guarding yourself with this protective shield will only isolate you from deeper connections and relationships. Authenticity and vulnerability go hand in hand when your actions and words reflect your values and beliefs accurately. Although vulnerability is often viewed as a weakness by people, it actually signifies great strength. It takes courage to openly express yourself and be honest and willingly expose to others who you really are.

Opening up and showing vulnerability can deepen existing connections with others and support growth by fostering emotional intimacy in relationships through sharing fears and dreams as well as insecurities with others. Forming a deeper bond beyond superficial interactions helps build trust and understanding between people. This closeness enriches relationships by enhancing self-awareness and self-worth only when you express genuine emotions openly. Embracing self-awareness leads to self-acceptance and self-love by accepting every part of yourself, including the flaws and imperfections; they are inklings that vulnerability fosters strength and bravery. In moments when you opt for vulnerability. you're arming yourself with the strength to confront obstacles with confidence. This endurance grants you the ability to navigate through the ups and downs in your life gracefully and resolutely.

Let's reflect on this story of Emma and Jack, a couple who was facing the possibility of drifting in their relationship due to unresolved tensions and emotional voids between them. In a counseling session, Jack took the step open up about his innermost insecurities and fear of failure. His candid revelation stirred emotions in Emma that brought tears to her eyes. In response to Jacks openness and honesty, Emma reciprocated with her admission of loneliness and feelings of inadequacy. This shared moment of vulnerability served as a turning point in their marriage dynamics. Their emotional bond grew stronger. They rediscovered the empathy and comprehension they had misplaced before. As a result, this led them to rebuild their relationship based on trust and mutual support.

Let me share now the story of Alex. Alex is someone who faced challenges in building connections with others due to keeping his feelings to himself to avoid criticism and exclusion. One particular day marked a change for Alex when he chose to open up to his friends by revealing a story of failure related to a business endeavor that deeply affected his confidence and sense of self-worth. To his amazement and relief, his friends responded with empathy by sharing their own stories of struggles. This act of vulnerability truly transformed the dynamics of their group by strengthening their bonds through mutual understanding and trust. Alex found as a result that their friendships deepened and became more authentic as they were based on shared moments and mutual encouragement.

Vulnerability can actually be a catalyst for personal development and progress. Take Sarah's trip as an example. She was a skilled but introverted worker who held back from sharing her ideas during team meetings because of fear of rejection. But, she was encourage by a mentor who believed in her potential. So, Sarah decided to step out of her comfort zone and present a project she deeply cared about despite feeling nervous and insecure. Her ideas were embraced positively by her colleagues who recognized her courage and passion. This experience not only boosted Sarah's self-confidence but also created new opportunities for advancement in her professional development. Embracing vulnerability enabled Sarah to progress in her career while also fostering a sense of self-worth and bravery, just as with Alex.

It is true also that the journey to vulnerability is also filled with fears and concerns that hold us back. Many people are scared of being rejected or judged; they think that being authentic and open about themselves will only result in criticism or being left alone, which is not necessarily true. This fear stems from past experiences where being vulnerable led to an unfavorable response. Some people fear to be seen as weak or inadequate. Living in a society that places a value on strength and too much on perfection, makes showing vulnerability seem like exposing a flaw. This mistaken belief that vulnerability equals fragility is what stops people from sharing their true selves, from opening up to others. There's also the fear of past traumas resurfacing and causing distress all over again. And yes, opening up about areas of your life can resurface painful memories and make it quite intimidating to do so, but it's worthy to conquer those fears.

To conquer fears, understand that vulnerability isn't just revealing or exposing recklessly, but being truthful and open to nurture connection and growth. Courage and a readiness to confront unease are essential in embracing your vulnerabilities. It's about believing that the rewards of deeper connections and personal growth surpass any risk. When you confront and deal with these fears, you can start embracing your vulnerabilities and unleash its life changing impact on your life.

EXERCISES TO EMBRACE VULNERABILITY

The journey of embracing vulnerability may seem intimidating at first; however, journaling also serves as a valuable tool to help you navigate this path effectively. Kickstart by remembering your encounters with vulnerability. Write down instances where you let your guard down and shared openly with others; ponder on how these moments influenced your relationships with others and your own self-perception. For instance, recall a moment when you confided in a friend about a personal struggle. Write about how did they react and how did you feel afterwards. Next, think about your fears and obstacles hindering your ability to be open hearted. Reflect on questions such as "Why do I feel hesitant to reveal my true self to others?" and "Which past events have shaped my current reluctance?" Also, think about how being vulnerable has positively influenced other people, and reflect on the narratives of those who have deepened their connections or undergone personal development by embracing their true selves. These anecdotes can demonstrate the importance of vulnerability and should inspire you to embrace it as well.

Gradually introducing yourself to vulnerability can be a way to open up more comfortably to others around you. To begin this journey towards openness, start by sharing personal details with someone close, with a friend or a colleague, talking about hobbies or interests. Notice how the conversation develops and their reaction. Taking steps like this in situations that are not high pressured is also effective. Try exposing your feelings in common conversations or admitting when you don't now something. These little actions will help you become more confident and make vulnerability seem less daunting. As time goes on, you can slowly increase how much you open up to others. As you start to feel at ease revealing details about yourself to others and feel ready for it, start sharing with a trusted friend more meaningful areas of your life in a safe environment as well sharing a personal struggle or opening up about your true feelings. This gradual approach can help you develop resilience and confidence in your capacity to show vulnerability.

Engaging in *role playing* activities provides a space to work on being open and genuine with others; in other words, to be vulnerable. Just picture yourself sharing something personal with a friend during in this roll-playing exercise. It's a chance to express your emotions and see how they respond with empathy and understanding. By participating in these role playing scenarios you can boost your ability to communicate openly about your feelings in real life situations. For example, you might practice addressing concerns or sharing your needs with a coworker or manager at work. Whether its seeking assistance on a project or voicing your opinions during a meeting, these exercises will help you become more comfortable with expressing vulnerability in such settings. Engaging in this role play scenario can assist you in navigating work environments with sincerity and transparency. You can also practice seeking assistance or support in a rehearsed manner by articulating your requirements whether it's to ask for help with a task or for support during challenging times. These interactive role playing exercises will be beneficial for easing your anxiety and preparing you for real life interactions.

Practicing *mindfulness* is key in handling anxiety when feeling vulnerable. Revisit Chapter 4 for some effective exercises. Leveraging breathing during these moments can keep you centered and relaxed. Focus your attention on your breath as you take deep inhales through your nose and exhale through your mouth. This straightforward practice can ground you and alleviate your anxiety feelings. The body scanning meditation we also mentioned in Chapter 4 is another method to identify the sensations of vulnerability in you. Lay down comfortably and focus your awareness from your toes up to your head. Without being critical of yourself, pay attention to any uncomfortable feelings that is bringing you tension. This approach can help you recognize how vulnerability shows up in your body and enable you to respond to it with care. It's important to practice self-kindness during mindfulness sessions. When you're engaged in mindfulness activities, you need to repeat to yourself that it's normal to feel vulnerable and that you are worthy of compassion and empathy. This habit encourages an inner dialogue that will make it easier to accept your vulnerability.

To enhance your path to embracing vulnerability further, you might want to try out a *reflective writing* activity. Take some time to write down your thoughts on a moment where you felt exposed or open. Share details about the event, your emotions at that time and what eventually happened as a result. Think about the lessons learned from that situation and how it influenced your relationships with others as well as how it impacted your self-perception. Engaging in this exercise will offer you perspectives and strengthen the rewarding facets of being vulnerable.

BUILDING TRUST IN RELATIONSHIPS

Belief in each others is what forms the basis of any relationship. Trusting someone means putting faith in their actions and words. It means believing that they have your interests at heart and will stay true to their commitments. Trust is what sets the stage for vulnerability to thrive by providing an environment for emotional openness. Building this foundation requires consistency and honesty. Keeping promises and behaving predictably reassures others that they can count on you. This reliability creates a feeling of safety for everyone involved to be themselves in relationships or interactions with others.

To establish trust within your connections with others effectively, you need to communicate openly and honestly right from the beginning. Share your thoughts, emotions, and needs and encourage your partner or friend to do the same without any fear of criticism. This type of communication helps build a foundation of mutual understanding. Furthermore. sustaining trust involves keeping promises and commitments. To demonstrate your trustworthiness, make sure to do what you say you will do. Consistency demonstrates your reliability and reinforces your trustworthiness. Additionally, taking the time to empathize and understand others are key factors. When someone shares their feelings or experiences, listen attentively, validate their emotions, and show concern. This deepens the connection and builds trust.

Engaging in trust-building activities can strengthen relationships between individuals or groups working towards a shared goal. Think of *trust falls* as an example. They are effective ways to enhance trust and teamwork dynamics. A trust fall involves one person closing their eyes and falling backward with the expectation that their partner will catch them. This physical interaction serves as a symbol of trust and collaboration. This exercise is widely used in therapy to build trust. Working together, as a team, towards a common objective, cultivates a sense of togetherness and interdependence among participants.

Restoring trust after it has been broken is possible but challenging. When trust is compromised, the initial step to rebuild trust involves recognizing the breach and taking responsibility. This means admitting your fault without making excuses. Offering an sincere apology is essential. A sincere apology should convey regret and a dedication to rectifying the situation. It's not about just saying "I'm sorry," but to demonstrate that you grasp the repercussions of your actions and are ready to make amends. In order to rebuild trust, you will need to demonstrate a dependable behavior over a period of time with actions rather than just words.

Trust is what holds relationships together. Building trust is like nurturing a bond that keeps the relationship intact and strong over time, with sincere dedication and consistent gestures of care and understanding even when its been shaken or damaged in the past. This is what allows relationships to grow.

SHARING YOUR TRUE SELF

Living authentically means staying true to your values and beliefs while ensuring that your actions and words mirror who you truly are as a person in every aspect of your life rather than only when it's convenient. Being authentic is closely tied to vulnerability because it entails being open and honest about who you're without kidding behind a mask. This level of honesty with yourself and those around you fosters deeper and meaningful relationships and inner peace. Being true to yourself is good for your wellbeing as it helps reduce the stress and anxiety that arise from pretending to be someone you're not. Improved relationships is another advantage as people tend to trust and relate to you more easily when you are genuine and sincere.

There are many factors today that can hinder individuals from expressing their true selves openly and honestly in society. On such factor are societal expectations and the apprehension of facing criticism or scrutiny from others, which can act as major deterrents to self-expression and authenticity for fear of not fitting in or standing out too much. This is why society dictates how we should behave, dress, and even think. All of this will result in internalized shame and self-doubt that will affect your thoughts. If you've faced criticism or rejection before in your life, you might find yourself holding on to those thoughts as you grow older; questioning your value and worrying that your true self may not measure up to these standards. Previous experiences of criticism or rejection can also leave behind lasting wounds causing you to feel reluctant to open up and be vulnerable again. These past experiences can form a barrier around your true self, but this often results in feelings of solitude and loneliness.

A good exercise to uncover your authentic self is practicing creative writing and storytelling as outlets for self-expression and reflection without worrying about criticism or judgment on you. You can start by writing about a significant event that influenced your growth and development. This will help you understand those experiences and embrace them as part of your authentic self. Another technique is to engage in art and music as mediums to self-expression. Engaging in activities like painting or playing music can help express emotions that words may struggle to convey. These creative pursuits serve as an avenue to explore your thoughts and expressing them to others in a meaningful way. Joining communities and sharing personal anecdotes can be empowering too. Seek out a group where you feel comfortable and respected to open up about your experiences. This act of sharing, not only aids in accepting your authentic self, but also fosters feelings of belonging and camaraderie.

It can be tough to show your true self to others at times, but the benefits are truly meaningful in many ways. Being authentic to who you're can result in stronger bonds with others and better acceptance of yourself – ultimately leading to a fulfilling life. Remember that as you uncover and accept your true self, it's all about self-discovery and growth. The next chapter will touch upon hands on activities for inner child healing – helping you take another step forward in understanding yourself and nurturing your emotional health. In the next chapter, we'll talk more in detail about art-therapy activities.

PRACTICAL EXERCISES FOR
INNER CHILD HEALING

*L*et's star by imagining yourself in a room with an empty notebook on the table and a pen ready in your hand. As you start writing, you notice that your thoughts and feelings flow effortlessly onto the page. Engaging in the practice of journaling can serve as a valuable method for inner child healing. Journal writing allows you to articulate emotions that may be challenging to put into words. It serves as a means of self-expression that invites insight and facilitates the release of emotions that are difficult to verbalize. When you put your thoughts on paper, you are creating a safe space where your inner child can open up and express all those hidden feelings and thoughts that were tucked away for so long.

GUIDED JOURNALING PROMPTS

Writing in a journal can be therapeutic and beneficial for nurturing and healing your inner child by serving as a mirror to reflect your deepest thoughts, emotions, and feelings onto paper. Expressing your feelings through writing can help untangle any knots within you by giving them structure and clarity. This kind of journaling is the act of putting words to your emotions and often provides a sense of release and understanding. Additionally, this practice of journaling has the potential to revealing layers of your inner self (aspects of your psyche) that you wouldn't even know existed. These hidden patterns in thoughts and actions can uncover the source of your emotional struggles. Uncovering the source leads to self-awareness and the first step towards healing and growth.

Here are some suggestions to assist you with your journal writing practice. Start by writing a letter to your inner child expressing love and support; picturing yourself speaking to the younger version of yourself and offering the kindness and reassurance you craved back then. Another helpful prompt is to describe a happy childhood memory and how it made you feel at the time. Revisiting positive moments can deepen your connection with your inner child and bring to light the happiness and innocence that remain within you. Next, think about a moment from your childhood when you felt hurt and consider what you needed at that time of vulnerability. This activity can aid in recognizing your needs so that you can start taking steps to meet those needs. Finally, write down the characteristics of your inner child that you cherish because these attributes can promote self-love and appreciation.

For this exercise to work, consistency plays an important role in this journal writing process. Allocate a time every day for this activity – whether its in the morning to kickstart your day with reflection or in the evening to relax and organize your thoughts. Maintaining this journal will help you monitor your emotional development allowing you to measure your growth and identify areas for improvement. Reviewing previous entries can offer valuable perspectives. You may observe themes or changes in your point of view that could guide you through your healing journey..

However, many people struggle when it comes to starting or maintaining a journaling habit due to writer's block issues. If you find yourself in this situation and feel stuck creatively during this process, try out freewriting methods to jumpstart the flow of your thoughts and ideas. You can set a timer for a period of five to ten minutes and write down whatever thoughts come to mind without worrying about grammar or structure. The main objective is to keep the ink flowing on paper and silence your inner critic during that time. Drawing inspiration from images or quotes can also help ignite your imagination and creativity during this process. Select an image that deeply connects with you or select a quote that resonates with your feelings and share whatever it brings to your mind. Changing your journal writing space with frequency can present a fresh perspective on things. Consider writing in another room or stepping outside or going to a café to observe how this changes in scenery impact your thoughts and reflections.

In summary, keeping a journal is a powerful way to heal your inner child by offering a secure outlet for self-expression and emotional exploration while also aiding in self-discovery and personal growth. By integrating journal writing into your routine and using prompts to spark your thoughts and reflections, you can promote a stronger connection with your inner child and uncover underlying emotions that influence your present day experiences. As you keep writing in your journal over time, you will discover that it becomes an ally on your journey towards healing and self-acceptance.

VISUALIZATION TECHNIQUES

Through visualization techniques, you open the door to your memories and have the opportunity to reframe them in a way that brings comfort and empowerment. By reframing your past, you create a safe and empowered environment for yourself, providing the care that may have been lacking in your childhood.

Practice this visualization technique. Begin by locating an cozy spot where you can unwind without any interruptions. Sit down comfortably or in a reclined position and initiate a guided visualization session by crafting a secure sanctuary (as safe space) for your inner child. Close your eyes and breathe deeply for a moment to release any stress you may be carrying. Envision a place that brings you comfort and serenity. Whether it's a beachscape or woodland area, or simply a snug room. Visualize every aspect of this place. Notice the details, the colors around you, the sounds, and scents that fill the air. Imagine yourself as a kid in this location. Take some time in this comforting environment and let yourself experience a sense of peace and safety.

Now, visualize a scenario where you meet you inner child and console your self. Then see yourself as you are at the present moment, then visualize your younger self in this safe place. Observe your inner child's reactions. Are they excited to see you or hesitant in any way? Sit down and engage with them by asking about their feelings, attentively listening to their responses without judgement. Provide words of support and encouragement assuring them that you are there to protect and stand by them. Engaging in this exchange may foster stronger connections with your inner child and attend to unresolved emotional needs.

Reparenting visualization is another effective strategy you can practice. In this exercise, you picture yourself as an supportive parent or caregiver for your inner child – offering them the love and encouragement they may lacked before. You may comfort them with words or sharing in activities that bring them joy. For example, if your inner child had a passion for drawing but never got the chance to explore it, visualize spending time with them sketching together. This reparenting process (the process of providing guidance) can aid in healing past wounds, nurturing feelings of safety and self-worth.

This practice of visualization is effective because it allows you to envision a healthier (healed) version of yourself without past burdens weighing you down. Take a moment to imagine your self living a happy and fulfilling life. See how you engage with others, pursue your interests, and prioritize self-care. These positive visualization can be super motivating and give you a clear vision of the goals you are striving for.

There are additional practices you can incorporate to enhance the effectiveness of these visualization exercises. For example, you can integrate calming music or natural sounds to create a soothing environment that promotes relaxation and deep engagement in the visualization process. Additionally, you can also incorporate breathing techniques both before and during each visualization exercise. Doing this will aid in soothing your nervous system and help you remain grounded in the current moment.

Her are some real-life situations that will demonstrate how visualization methods have had a significant effect on people's lives. Michael, for example, found solace in envisioning himself comforting and safeguarding his inner child regularly, which helped him let go of feelings of shame and self-doubt over time. He mentioned feeling a boost in confidence and self -belief in his current interactions. Sarah is a career driven individual who made visualization a part of her self-care routine. Every morning she dedicated a moment to visualize her future self leading a fulfilling life. This routine set a positive tone for the day and helped her stay committed to her goals towards healing.

ART THERAPY ACTIVITIES

Practicing art therapy offers a way to heal your inner child through a non-verbal form of expression as opposed to traditional therapy. This non-verbal creative process helps you connect deeply with your emotions by activating areas of your brain that are more in tune with feelings and creativity, the right side of your brain. It allows you to connect with your feelings and communicate emotions that may be challenging to put into words. Being creative and playful in activities can have a profound healing power by allowing you to rediscover the pure and happy essence of your inner child. Creating art becomes a safe place for your inner child where it can express itself without any judgement.

A very effective art therapy practice is drawing or painting a portrait of your inner child and how you see yourself. Begin by imagining yourself as a child and then sketch that image on paper using colors and shapes that represent your emotions and memories. But don't stress about your abilities, just aim to depict the core essence of your inner child. Another impactful practice is crafting a collage that reflects your childhood experiences. You can collect magazines newspapers and various materials to cut out images and words that connect with your past experiences. Put the items on a sheet of paper to narrate your story differently, which might reveal insights into your childhood and uncover hidden emotions.

Another art therapy tool is sculpting or molding with clay which provides a hands on method to convey your inner child's emotions creatively. Shape the clay with your hands to create figures that reflect the feelings of your inner child. The process of shaping and molding can be therapeutic as you let go off your emotions. You can also use colored clay to represent your emotions with different colors. For example, red could denote anger, blue might represent sadness, and yellow could represent joy. Use all these colors to create abstract art to capture and express your current emotional state. After this practice, you will understand better your emotions.

The healing aspect of art is in the process, not the art itself. For this reason, you should concentrate on expressing your emotions rather than creating a master piece. The goal is to connect with your feelings and translate them into a tangible form, art. For this to work, you need to allow your emotions to flow, and if you're sad or angry, let those feelings influence your creative output. Once done, you can reflect on your artwork, examine what you've created, and reflect upon what it might reveal about your inner child. Ask yourself: "What emotions are more prominent in my art piece?" This reflection will deepen your understanding about you inner child and will help in your inner healing process.

Starting with art therapy for beginners might feel overwhelming to some. Just start by collecting materials you think you would enjoy using; art supplies like paper, markers, paint, clay, etc. Anything that will spark your creativity. Find in your home a cozy area where you won't be disturbed. Put aside any self-criticism; just enjoy the creative process. Give yourself the freedom to create without worrying on the end result. Remember that the process is more important than the resulting art piece.

You can use prompts to guide your creative process in the right direction. For example, you could start off with a prompt such as "Imagine and draw your inner child in their favorite place" or "Create a sculpture that represents your current emotional state." Prompts like these serve as a starting point and they can assist you in digging deeper into your artistic expression. Don't be afraid to explore different styles and mediums to find what truly speaks to you – whether its, through painting, collage, creating a sculpture, or even digital art creations. Every form of media provides an avenue for expressing your feelings.

In conclusion, engaging in art therapy provides an easy way to connect with your inner child by expressing yourself creatively to explore deep emotions and gain insights into your life experiences, both past and present. Making art is therapeutic on its own as it allows your inner child a safe place for self expression.

ROLE-PLAYING SCENARIOS

Role-playing is a another therapy practice or tool that allows you to experience different scenarios and gain emotional clarity through exploration and expression of various perspectives and feelings from your past experiences in child-hood. You will be able to analyze several scenarios from different perspectives. With role-playing, you'll able to address and work through emotions that might have been buried for years, which can be intense because you'll be confronting and processing those past feelings.

Imagine a role playing scenario where you interact with your inner child through a conversation setting. You start the dialog face to face with your inner child by inquiring about how they feel and what they need. This activity can offer valuable insights revealing unfulfilled needs and lingering emotions. Another powerful scenario is a role playing of conversation between you as an adult and your parents or caregivers, allowing yourself to express suppressed feelings and thoughts from your childhood years. It's like when you finally sit down with your parents and share how their past actions have impacted you. Letting out those bottled-up feelings can feel freeing and bring a sense of resolution.

There is another exercise called *enacting scenario* which involves imagining a scenario where your inner self gets the care that was needed but didn't get. For example, if you lacked affection during your childhood, you can visualize and play a scenario where your inner self receives abundant love and attention. It's also important to be assertive during these role playing scenarios. Try enacting scenarios where you establish boundaries or advocate for yourself effectively. Engaging in these activities can help boost your confidence and get you ready for real life situations where standing up for yourself is crucial. You may want to consider teaming up with a friend or counselor to make these role playing exercises even more effective and encouraging. Adding props or simple costumes can enhance the experience, making it feel more real. For example, using a toy to represent your inner child or using a chair to depict a parental figure can have a huge impact. After role playing, your next step is to reflect on your feelings and knowledge you've acquired during the role playing activity. Lastly, write in your journal about the emotions felt during role playing. This reflection will solidify what you have learned and reinforce your healing process.

In summary, role playing scenarios is an effective way to connect with your inner child and work through past traumas. They are very effective because you can gain new perspectives and release any past trauma. Don't forget that these activities are meant to help you in reconnecting with your inner child and reshaping your emotional world.

HOLISTIC HEALING APPROACHES

There are many holistic approach or techniques to help you heal you inner child. The goal of these practices is to unite your physical wellbeing to your mental wellbeing. Some of these practices are meditation, tai chi, relaxation, and breathing exercises. Let's look into some of these holistic healing approaches.

INTEGRATING MIND-BODY PRACTICES

Mind-body techniques are methods designed to establish a link between your mental and physical wellbeing. With these techniques, you can achieve a state of balance that promotes both emotional and physical health awareness. Mind-body practices acknowledge that your mental state can affect your physical health. For example, when you are under stress and anxiety, it may translate into physical manifestations such as headaches and muscle tension. On the other hand, physical relaxation plays a role in calming the mind and reducing anxiety while fostering emotional equilibrium.

Adding mind body techniques to your schedule can reduce your stress and anxiety levels. Meditation, for example, serves as a method to soothe the mind and encourage a sense of calmness. Research has indicated that practicing meditation as a habit can lower cortisol levels—the hormone related to stress—and enhance emotional control. These benefits enable you to handle situations with balance composure. Tai chi is a type of martial art that combines slow and intentional motions with deep breathing. It can boost your balance and flexibility as well as sharpening your mental focus and emotional strength. Breathing exercises where you consciously regulate your breathing patterns can swiftly ground you and alleviate any anxiety you may have.

Incorporating mind body exercises into your routine will help you achieve a balanced state of wellbeing that boosts both your mental and physical wellbeing. The advantages of mind-body practices manifest gradually. For this reason, you must incorporate them to your routine. Refer back to Chapter 4 on how to practice these breathing techniques.

YOGA FOR TRAUMA RECOVERY

Yoga practice is a healing method that is especially beneficial for recovering from trauma situations. Yoga combines physical postures, breathing techniques, and meditation to cultivate a profound bond between the mind and body to regain control over your body by improving its awareness and your emotions. Engaging in deliberate movements while focusing on your breathing will help you connect with how your body feels without any kind of pressure. The improvement of your awareness will facilitate the release of your emotions, allowing you to process your trauma and let go of it. Another benefit from Yoga practice is that it helps reducing stress by helping to lower cortisol levels , promoting relaxation and emotional resilience. Cortisol is the hormone responsible of managing how the body responds to stress.

Trauma-sensitive yoga (TSY) is a style of yoga tailored to provide a nurturing and secure space for people who have gone through traumatic experiences. Unlike traditional yoga where there is a set structure to follow, TSY prioritizes giving you the freedom to choose and control the practice. You're encouraged to tune into your body's needs and choose movements that resonate with you, what feels good to you, without feeling obligated to conform to any particular pose or sequence. This emphasis on autonomy is especially valuable for those healing from trauma as it helps them rebuild their trust in their body as well as their decisions. Another advantage is that TSY also integrates elements of mindfulness and self-care practices to aid in recovery by encouraging you to focus on the present moment and treating yourself with kindness. This way, you can start healing past emotional wounds within a supportive class setting where safety and comfort are prioritized and all these with the support of instructors equipped to effectively support anyone experiencing distress signals.

Let's discuss now about some yoga positions that can help in recovering from trauma. *Child's Pose*, for example, is a grounding posture that fosters a feeling of safety and stability. To do this pose, kneel on a mat with your your big toes touching each other and the knees apart. Then, stretch your arms out in front and rest your head gently on the mat. This posture aids in easing tension in the shoulders as well as the back while promoting a sense of calmness and security.

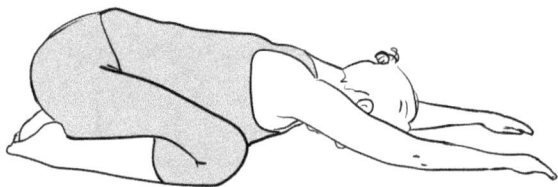

The next pose is the *Bridge Pose*, which is also great for emotional release. Lie down on your back with your knees bent and feet resting flat on the mat. Press your feet against the mat and gently lift your hips upward towards the ceiling to create a bridge shape with your body. This posture helps to open up your chest and heart region while also aiding in the release of any bottled up emotions.

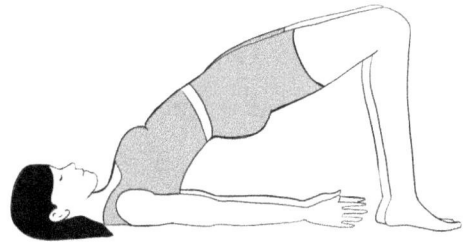

Next, we have the *Legs-Up-The-Wall Pose*, which is particularly beneficial for promoting relaxation and stress relief. Start by sitting to a wall with one side of your body touching it; then smoothly extend your legs up against the wall as you recline into a comfortable position. Relax your arms down. Pay attention to your breathing while practicing this pose which helps soothe the nerves and will induce a profound sense of calmness and relaxation within you.

Getting into yoga might feel overwhelming at first, especially if you're working through trauma; but finding a yoga class or a trauma-sensitive instructor can be a good start! Look for classes labeled as "trauma-sensitive" or "trauma-informed" to make sure you're in a supportive environment. If going to classes in person isn't possible for you at the moment, there are plenty of online resources and videos available to help you explore trauma-sensitive yoga practices at your own speed.

Begin by dedicating a few minutes every day to your practice and gradually increase the time as you become comfortable with it. Remember that consistency is crucial; so, establishing a regular routine is key. Set up a dedicated area for your yoga sessions – make sure it's peaceful and distraction free so you can feel secure and relaxed during your practice. A tranquil spot could just be a nook in a room featuring a yoga mat and soothing items such as candles or gentle music.

In summary, enhancing body awareness, facilitating emotional release, and reducing stress levels are some of the key benefits of yoga, especially when you are trying to recover from trauma. Through yoga sessions you will regain a connection with your body and learn to trust yourself again while nurturing feelings of inner peace and resilience.

THE ROLE OF NUTRITION IN EMOTIONAL HEALING

Think about starting your day with a bowl of berries, nuts, and a dollop of creamy yogurt. It can have a positive impact on your mood and wellbeing throughout the day! The link between our food choices and how we feel is indeed significant. What we eat plays a role in maintaining good mental and emotional health too. It's important to note that our brain relies on an intake of essential nutrients to function at its best level possible! Omega-3 fatty acids sources like salmon, chia seeds, walnuts, and flaxseeds are particularly beneficial in this regard as they not only support brain function but also help in stabilizing emotions by reducing inflammation and promoting effective communication between brain cells. Eating diets rich in sugar and processed foods can have a negative impact on our mood and mental wellbeing as they may lead to mood swings and anxiety while also contributing to depression through inflammation and disruptions in brain function.

To maintain your wellbeing in check, here are a few uncomplicated yet wholesome meal ideas for you to try out!

- Kickstart your morning routine with a smoothie with mood-boosting ingredients. Blend a mixture of fresh spinach leaves with a banana and some frozen berries and toss in a sprinkle of flax seeds before pouring in some almond milk – all into the blender! This delightful blend not offers a burst of antioxidants and fiber but also serves as a rich source of Omega-3 fatty acids that can help balance your emotions and energize your day.

- For a lunch or dinner, consider a salad with mixed leafy greens and nutritious fats for nourishment and enjoyment! Mix together an assortment of greens with slices of creamy avocado and juicy cherry tomatoes along with refreshing cucumber, and a handful of nuts or seeds for crunchiness and flavor enhancement. Give it a drizzle of olive oil and a splash of tangy lemon juice to elevate the overall taste experience into something truly delightful and satisfying for your palates pleasure. The combination of avocado and nuts not adds richness but also provides essential nutrients that promote brain health; meanwhile, the vibrant greens contribute an array of vital vitamins and minerals for your overall wellbeing.

- Another comforting choice for you. A soup recipe featuring anti-inflammatory ingredients. Begin by heating up onions, garlic and ginger in oil until they're fragrant and deliciously golden brown. Toss in some finely chopped carrots and sweet potatoes along with a sprinkle of turmeric before pouring in vegetable broth to let all the flavors mingle harmoniously. Allow the mixture to simmer gently until the vegetables turn soft and tender to the touch. Then, carefully blend everything together until you achieve a velvety creamy texture that is sure to warm both your body and soul. The added benefits of turmeric and ginger will work their magic to help combat inflammation. Sweet potatoes and carrots contain an amount of beta-carotene that helps in maintaining brain health and boosting your immune system.

Embracing a mindful approach to eating can amplify the advantages of maintaining a healthy diet regimen. Take your time enjoying each morsel of food to fully appreciate its flavors and textures. This mindful eating technique promotes satisfaction and reduces the risk of overeating. It's important to tune in to your body's signals of hunger and fullness. Honor your hunger by eating when you feel it and stop when you're contentedly full. As a result, you'll cultivate a positive relationship with your food and steer clear of emotional eating habits.

Creating ambience while eating is equally important. Arrange your table thoughtfully when dining solo. Eliminate distractions such as television or mobile phones. Concentrate on the dining experience. This exclusive moment lets you engage with your food and value the nourishment it offers. You should also consider maintaining a food diary to monitor the impact of foods on your wellbeing on how it makes yo feel. Record any shifts in your emotions, vitality, or digestion. This can assist you in recognizing foods that enhance your health and those that may be advisable to avoid.

ENCOURAGING DEEP SELF-REFLECTION

*I*magine admiring the starry night sky, each twinkle reflecting a thought in your mind; a tranquil evening allowing for introspection and deep contemplation. This serene moment holds the potential for self-reflection, much like how the stars serve as guiding spotlights in the darkness to lead you through the intricate maze of your innermost thoughts and emotions. Engaging in what's known as *Socratic questioning* is a powerful way for you to undergo profound self-reflection as it stems from ancient philosophies and encourages questioning assumptions and nurturing critical thinking skills.

SOCRATIC QUESTIONING TECHNIQUES

Socratic questioning is a form of disciplined questioning that serves various purposes by guiding contemplation in diverse directions and for many purposes. It was named after the

Greek philosopher Socrates since he developed it. The goal of this discipline is to spark discussions by questioning the person's beliefs and promoting insights into concepts. Through a series of open ended questions, Socrates sought to foster analytical thinking and shed light on notions that had not been considered before. This approach has now been used in a range of areas such as education and training programs, as well as counseling and mentoring sessions for its proven ability to cultivate self-awareness and understanding.

Socratic questioning is more about challenging assumptions and beliefs than offering solutions by asking the right questions that prompt self-exploration and discovery of underlying beliefs influencing our mindset and actions. Through scrutinizing these beliefs, we can distinguish between those that support our progress and those that impede it. This approach nurtures thinking by urging us to explore diverse viewpoints and assess the validity of our assumptions and also encourages self-reflection by aiding us in comprehending the underlying reasons or motivations for our actions and thoughts.

The following are some of the Socratic questions that can help you explore your thoughts and beliefs effectively. One important questions is: "What proof do I have that validates this conviction?" This question encourages you to scrutinize the foundation of your beliefs and assists in distinguishing between what is real and what is merely presumed. Another stimulating question is: "How could I be wrong about my assessment?" This question lets you answer with humility and adaptability by helping you explore other perspectives and acknowledge the limitations of your own perspectives. Asking yourself "What outcomes result from maintaining this belief?" will help you understand how your beliefs can influence your decisions, actions, and overall wellbeing. Asking yourself questions such as "Who else has a different perspective than mine, and why?" prompt you to entertain different perspectives fostering empathy and to amplify your understanding.

The advantages of using Socratic questioning are numerous and diverse in nature and scope. This method fosters mindedness and adaptability (being flexible), qualities that are crucial for personal development. By questioning your beliefs and viewpoints regularly, you can cultivate a mindset that is more receptive and open towards new ideas. Socratic questioning also plays a role in recognizing and challenging limiting beliefs that hinder your progress. By scrutinizing these beliefs, you can replace them with more empowering beliefs, which subsequently leads you towards positive changes in your attitudes and actions. As a result, you will be boosting your emotional intelligence and improving your relationships with others.

A good exercise is to write in your journal about your beliefs and question those beliefs using the sample questions mentioned previously. Also, look for supporting evidence for those beliefs. This practice could uncover new perspectives you didn't consider before.

Feel free sharing your ideas and beliefs with any close friend or therapist and encourage them to ask you Socratic questions. This exercise can reveal assumptions and help you discover better ways of handling the issue.

In summary, by integrating Socratic questioning into your self-reflection routines, you have the opportunity to discover deeper layers of self-awareness and personal development.

REFLECTION JOURNALS

We talked earlier about journaling. In this section, we'll talk specifically about reflection journals.

Keeping a reflection journal can be a means of navigating your thoughts and emotions, enabling you to express ideas that may otherwise linger unvoiced and tangled within you. This consistent process will provide clarity to your inner world deepening your understanding of your emotions as a way to enhance self-awareness and personal growth over time. This journal will capture your development and document the valuable insights you acquire through the process.

There are several benefits you can acquire form journaling.

- It can provide a safe space to express your emotions without fear of criticism and to release feelings you've been holding in you.

- Writing down your thoughts and looking at them

with fresh eyes can help you process your thoughts better and find resolution.

- Maintaining a journal will help you monitor your personal development by uncovering recurring patterns and common themes in your life experiences.

- Review your past entries to pinpoint areas where you have progressed and those that still need some work.

This continues self-reflection will help you create a feeling of growth and progress through your journey, making it tangible.

Some questions to consider are: "What did I learn about myself today?" "How did I handle a recent challenging situation?" "What are my recent successes and what have they thought me?" These questions will encourage you to research into your feelings and understand their origins.

To make journaling more effective and impactful, it's important to use techniques that enhance its value. One key approach is to write without holding back or censoring yourself, letting your thoughts flow naturally without being concerned about perfect grammar or structure. This method of freewriting aims to help you access insights from your subconscious mind more easily. Furthermore, using language to convey your emotions and experiences can also add depth and meaning to your journal entries. Detail how you're feeling using words that bring your experiences vividly to life on paper. Lastly, it's beneficial to revisit past entries from time to time for reflection and further insight into your journey. When reflecting on the experiences and feelings you've had, you may notice recurring trends or patterns in your actions and emotions.

To illustrate how you could approach your journal writing routine, here are a couple of examples of journal entries. One entry could focus on a disagreement and the insights gained from it – like this: "Today, I had a disagreement with my friend over a misunderstanding situation that initially made me defensive; but as we talked, I realized I was projecting my own insecurities, which made me understand the importance of acknowledging and openly discussing my emotions." Another entry might capture a moment and its impact: "This morning I walked through the park. Was filled with a deep sense of tranquility as the sun warmed my face and the birds sang around me. A gentle reminder to cherish life's little joys." Another instance could be about reaching a milestone and the path taken to achieve it. "After months of intense training sessions, I finally conquered my first marathon challenge. The journey was tough. Crossing that finish line brought immense satisfaction and taught me valuable lessons about determination and goal setting."

I encourage you to keep journal of reflections as a habit for self-discovery and personal development as it will allow you to organize your thoughts and emotions, gain perspective and understanding, and monitor your progress.

EXPLORING YOUR EMOTIONAL STATE

Our emotional state and your feelings are shaped by our past experiences in life. For example, a strong sense of fear may be connected to a past traumatic event, whereas happiness could be associated with a fond memory. By exploring these connections, you can gain insight into how your past experiences impact or influence your emotional wellbeing. Having this awareness empowers you to manage your feelings and respond thoughtfully in any situation.

You can explore your emotions with the *emotion wheel* which is a tool that will assist you in recognizing and naming your feelings accurately by categorizing them into primary and secondary emotions. This makes it simpler to determine the exact emotions you are dealing with. For example, starting with a feeling such as anger and then digging deeper into more precise emotions like frustration or resentment, allows for a better understanding of your emotional complexity. It's important to identify these emotions in order to gain insights into your emotional state. By taking a moment to sit quietly in a setting and tuning into your emotions without any bias or criticism help you notice your feelings as they emerge naturally and deal with them before they become too intense. Another useful method is performing a *body scan*. Refer to Chapters 4 and 6 on how use this mindfulness practice.

Before judging yourself when exploring your emotions, first ask yourself: "What is the reason behind this feeling?" This simple question can lead your emotions on a deeper level. You can simply try to observe and accept them. Allow yourself to experience those emotions without holding back. This method foster a healthier relationship with your emotional state, helping you navigate it efficiently.

An impactful activity is to *write letters to each of your emotions.* For example, you can write a letter to your anxiety, expressing how it makes you feel. This exercise will help you externalize your emotions and, as a result, you'll understand those emotions better. Keep track of these emotion in your journal. With time, you will notice some similar patterns that will help you understand your emotional state.

GAINING INSIGHTS THROUGH SELF-REFLECTION

Standing at a crossroads can be quite perplexing when you're unsure about which direction to choose. We all face moments when we need to make decisions, and gaining insights is like finding a guiding map that will help move forward. Insights serve as eye opening realizations about ourselves. Those 'aha' moments that suddenly illuminate the complexity of our emotions or actions. Understanding why we react in certain ways or hold specific beliefs can trigger positive shifts in how we behave and think. This insight will help you break old bad habits and transform them into healthier habits. You will learn to understand what you need.

To help you gain insights about your thinking patterns, I recommend you to exercise *self-reflection* asking yourself reflective question after a significant event. You can ask your-self questions like: "What was I really feeling during that argument?" and "What underlying needs or fears were driving my reactions?" Our dreams often reveal parts of our minds and feelings that we may not be consciously aware of during the day; but writing down your dreams in a journal and exploring any recurring themes, might help you discover hidden aspects of yourself that needs attention. You'll be surprised also of how much insight can you gain when you share your thought with someone you trust that will listen without criticizing you. This can lead you to see things from a new angle.

As you continue to reflect and gain insights, you will discover you are more in harmony with your true self and will be ready to embrace the next steps towards your healing journey.

CULTIVATING SELF-LOVE AND SELF-WORTH

*H*aving a sense of self worth means that you understand your value as an individual from within yourself rather than relying solely on external achievements or other people's perceptions like self esteem does. It involves acknowledging and appreciating your worth – the fundamental belief that you matter regardless of what you achieve or how others sees you. This conviction plays a role in maintaining your emotional health by influencing how you treat and care for yourself and how you allow others to treat you. You will be able to focus more on making choices that bring you happiness and fulfillment.

BUILDING SELF-WORTH

Having a sense of self worth means that you understand your value as an individual from within yourself rather than relying solely on external achievements or other people's perceptions like self esteem does. It involves acknowledging and appreciating your worth – the fundamental belief that you matter regardless of what you achieve or how others sees you. This conviction plays a role in maintaining your emotional health by influencing how you treat and care for yourself and how you allow others to treat you. You will be able to focus more on making choices that bring you happiness and fulfillment.

There are several factors that influence your sense of self-worth and they start with your childhood experiences and parental influences. The messages you received from your parents or caregivers when you were young about self-worth will impact how you view yourself as an adult. For example, constant criticism or lack of affection can lead to feelings of inadequacy. On the other hand, being praised and encouraged can foster a strong sense of self-worth. Other factors are societal and cultural expectations. Society often places value on certain achievements, appearances, or behaviors, which can affect how you perceive your worth. While successes will boost your confidence, failures can sometimes lead to self-doubt. In relationships and social interactions, supportive relationships can enhance your self-worth, whereas toxic or abusive relationships will diminish it.

You can evaluate yourself by asking questions like "Do I perceive myself as deserving of love and respect?" or "Do I frequently compare myself to others and feel inadequate?" Create a *behaviors checklist* where you can record moments of low or high self-worth. Some indicators of having low self-esteem might include frequent self-criticism, avoiding challenges due to fear of failure, or seeking constant validation from others. In contrast, behaviors that reflect high self-worth include setting healthy boundaries, pursuing personal interests, and practicing self-compassion.

Boosting your self-esteem requires taking actions that you can integrate into your everyday routine. First, set feasible objectives that resonate with your principles and passions and that are reachable within a reasonable period of time. Reaching these milestones can enhance your assurance. Strengthen your perception of self-worth. Celebrate wins and achievements as you progress. Recognizing and appreciating your advancements no matter how insignificant they may appear is essential for cultivating a self-perception. Showing kindness and forgiveness to yourself is another step to take in your journey towards self-improvement. Be gentle and understanding towards yourself just as you would be with a friend. When you slip up or make a mistake of being hard on yourself, see it as a chance to learn and grow with kindness.

Boosting your self-esteem requires taking actions that you can integrate into your everyday routine. Start by setting realistic and achievable goals. Your goals should be aligned with your values and interests, and they should be attainable within a reasonable timeframe. When you achieve these goals it will boost your confidence and reinforce your self-esteem. Celebrate every time you reach a milestone. Recognizing and honoring your progress, no matter how small it may seem, is important for building a positive self-image. Another essential step is practicing self-compassion and forgiveness. Treat yourself with the same kindness and understanding that you would offer your friend. When you make a mistake, instead of criticizing yourself, think of it as a learning opportunity and just move forward.

Surround yourself people who support you, with positive influences than can also enhance your self-worth. Consider seeking professional help if you struggle with low self-esteem. A therapist can provide you with additional strategies to build and maintain a healthy sense of self-worth.

Remember that building self-esteem is a journey that involves caring for and appreciating yourself as you would tend to a garden. It takes time, dedication, and perseverance.

AFFIRMATION-BUILDING GUIDES

Starting each day by reminding yourself of the words "I deserve love and respect" will have a powerful impact on your mindset and wellbeing. Research into the effectiveness of affirmations reveals that these positive statements have the ability to rewire your brain's pathways by creating new neural connections. The continuous practice of positive self-talk exercises will trigger specific brain regions connected to self-esteem and pleasure processing that will gradually fuel positivity within you for lasting effects. Studies have indicated that positive affirmations have the potential to lower stress levels and enhance wellness while boosting overall happiness and contentment in life.

To create your affirmations, start by recognizing the negative self-perceptions or self-beliefs you wish to change – those inner dialogues that chip away at your self-assurance and value. Then, modify those beliefs into positive affirmations expressed in the present tense. For example, if the recurring thought is " I am not good enough" switch it up with "I am capable and worthy." Remember to make your affirmations precise and emotionally impactful. Your affirmations should mirror your true desires and values to have a greater impact on you. Here are some powerful affirmations to consider: "I deserve happiness," "My unique qualities make me special," and "I have the power to overcome any challenge."

Start incorporating affirmations in your daily routine to amplify their effectiveness. Begin your day by looking at yourself in the mirror and saying your affirmations aloud. This habit will not only strengthen the positive statements but will also establish a favorable atmosphere for the rest of your day. At night, take a moment to recollect your affirmations before going to sleep to let them seep into your subconscious mind. Jotting down affirmations, in a diary can also prove helpful. Set aside a portion of your journal for daily affirmations and commit to jotting them down every day as a routine practice to strengthen their influence on you further. Additionally, consider recording these affirmations to play them back repeatedly to enhance their effectiveness. You can use your phone or any other recording device to compile a collection of your affirmations and listen to them during your commute or when relaxing at home.

I understand you might be skeptical at the beginning of this affirmation routine. It's quite common to feel uncertain about whether affirmations really work, especially if you've been battling with negative self-beliefs for a while. To tackle this doubt, start first with affirmations that resonate with you. Over time, as you cultivate confidence in the process, you can incorporate more complex and emotionally charged affirmations into your routine. Additionally, combining visualization techniques with affirmations will amplify their effectiveness. When you say your affirmations again and again, try closing your eyes and picturing yourself living out those affirmations in a positive way. Think about the emotions, behaviors, and results associated with your affirmations. This mix can really influence your thoughts and emotions.

EMPOWERMENT EXERCISES

When you feel empowered, you believe in your ability to influence circumstances and make decisions that are in line with your values. This sense of control is linked to self-efficacy, which is the belief in your ability to succeed in specific situations. Empowerment increases your self-esteem by reinforcing the idea that you are capable and deserving of success and will help you feel in control and motivated to achieve your goals.

Visualization is one of the most effective exercises for empowerment. To practice this type of exercise, you must imagine yourself achieving a personal goal. For example, close your eyes and imagine every detail of the achievement. Feel the emotions of success, pride and joy. This mental rehearsal will help you build the confidence you need to pursue your goals.

Another very effective exercise is to act out situations in which you assert yourself. For example, choose a situation in which you feel insecure or passive and practice responding assertively using clear and confident language. Over time, these practices will make it easier for you to assert yourself in real-life situations.

Another exercise is to *write yourself a letter from your future self.* In this letter, you imagine that you have already achieved your goals and overcome your challenges, describe the journey, the lessons learned and the strength gained. This exercise will help you connect with your future potential and provide motivation for your current efforts. Practicing decision making in low-risk situations like this can also reinforce your autonomy. You can start with small decisions, such as what to have for dinner or what route to take to work, for example. Gradually you will make more important decisions with confidence and become more and more confident over time.

Keep in mind that taking action is crucial in the training process. Setting and pursuing your personal goals will give you a sense of direction and purpose in your life. Break big goals into smaller steps so that they are manageable and avoid feeling overwhelmed. It is also important to take responsibility for your decisions and actions. You must acknowledge your mistakes and learn from them instead of blaming external factors that influenced them. Participate in activities that challenge you and inspire growth. This could be learning a new skill, taking on a new project at work, or stepping out of your comfort zone in social situations. Each challenge faced and overcome will reinforce your sense of autonomy.

Empowerment can lead to major changes in your life. In Sarah's case, for example, she was stuck in a job that made her unhappy. She felt unfulfilled. After participating in empowerment exercises and focusing on clear goals, she took the courageous step of changing careers. This decision transformed her life, leading to greater job satisfaction and personal fulfillment. Empowerment is not just about achieving external success, but about feeling confident and in control of your life. It is about recognizing your worth and taking actions that are in line with your true self.

These empowerment exercises can make a real impact on your self-esteem and overall wellbeing. Visualization, role-playing, writing letters to your future self and practicing decision making are all effective ways to encourage empowerment. Taking proactive steps, setting goals, and challenging yourself further reinforce this sense of control. You can cultivate a strong sense of autonomy and self-esteem by incorporating these practices.

NURTURING YOURSELF DAILY

Every morning when you wake up and sense a readiness to tackle the day ahead it's like a soothing ritual that sets the tone for your day ahead. Taking time for self-care and nurturing regularly plays a role in cultivating self-love as it serves as a dedication to your wellbeing. By incorporating self care routines into your life you're signaling to both your mind and body that you deserve kindness and consideration. By staying committed to this belief system of self-worth and acknowledging your value and worthiness of love and kindness helps strengthen your sense of self-esteem.

Think about waking up every morning and feeling a sense of calm and readiness to face the day. This feeling stems from the daily practice of self-care. Taking care of yourself and nurturing yourself regularly is key to maintaining self-love because it acts as a commitment to yourself. When you practice self-care, you are actually sending your mind and body the powerful message that you deserve care and attention. This commitment will help you rebuild your self-esteem by reinforcing this idea.

Daily care can take many forms, from simple acts of relaxation to involving yourself in hobbies that bring you joy. Meditation is a powerful tool for calming your mind and centering yourself. Even a few minutes of mindful meditation a day can help reduce stress and increase your emotional resilience. Hobbies such as painting and writing, as we mentioned earlier, or playing a musical instrument can provide you with a creative outlet to express your emotions and explore your interests. Also, physical activities such as yoga or nature walks not only improve physical health, but also improve mood and energy levels. Practices such as taking a hot bath, reading a good book, or listening to relaxing music can help you unwind and relax.

Recognizing that errors and obstacles are part of everyone's journey underscores the importance of treating ourselves with grace during moments. Embracing self-kindness on a daily basis can be as simple as taking short breaks to offer ourselves comforting words and support. Practicing self-talk involves replacing self critical thoughts with encouraging and affirming statements like shifting from "Oops! I made a mistake again" to "Every experience helps in my growth and learning journey."

When you treat yourself with kindness and understanding, you will be cultivating your own emotional wellbeing. Self-compassion involves recognizing that everyone, including you, makes mistakes and experiences setbacks, and it is also imperative to be kind to yourself in those moments. Practicing self-compassion on a daily basis can include taking self-compassion breaks where you take time to reflect, encourage yourself, and say kind words to yourself. The act of speaking positively to yourself is known as positive self-talk. Positive self-talk is the technique of substituting self-critical thoughts for supportive and affirming phrases. For example, instead of saying "I screwed up again," you can say, "I am learning and growing from my experiences."

To make daily self-care a consistent habit, you can create a structured self-care plan. Start by setting aside specific times each day for these self-care activities. This could be in the morning, during a lunch break, or before bedtime. Setting aside a designated time will ensure that self-care becomes a regular part of your routine. During this time, also reflect on the impact of these practices on your self-esteem by journaling these experiences and noting any positive changes in your mood and outlook. This reflection will reinforce the benefits you gain from self-care and motivate you to continue to prioritize your own wellbeing. Please, take seriously the journaling exercises. I can't emphasize enough how important this practice is in the healing process. Most people are too lazy and fail to analyze themselves while practicing journaling. Don't be one of them.

Remember that when you reinforce this belief that you are valuable and deserving of love and kindness it will lead to the deepest feeling of self-love and satisfaction.

SUSTAINING YOUR HEALING JOURNEY

Like plants, your emotional wellbeing requires constant care and attention in order to thrive. Just as gardeners follow a routine to nurture their plants, you must establish a structured healing routine for lasting emotional growth and stability. A routine provides predictability and creates a sense of security and control in your life and it helps you establish positive habits that support your long-term emotional health.

CREATING A HEALING ROUTINE

To take care of your emotional health, be well and feel good inside and out every day, it is important that you formulate a healing schedule so that you can effectively manage stress and in turn develop healthy habits that contribute to your emotional wellbeing. These habits will eventually become part of your daily life which will facilitate a balanced and satisfying lifestyle. Following a routine will also give you a sense of security and predictability, especially when it comes to the ups and downs of the healing process. This is a structure that you can rely on to keep you focused and attentive during those difficult times.

Developing a personalized healing routine begins with assessing your individual needs and priorities. That's why you should take some time to reflect on what aspects of your life require the most attention. Ask yourself if you have anxiety issues, if you need more physical activity, or are seeking creative expression. Identifying your primary needs will guide you in creating a routine that addresses your particular circumstances. Once you've identified those needs, you are ready to set realistic and achievable goals. Start small, focusing on changes that are manageable for you and that you can build upon. For example, if you've never meditated before, then start with five minutes a day and increase the duration as you become more comfortable.

Physical exercise, whether it's running in the morning, practicing yoga or attending dance classes, improves mood and energy levels. Creative expression through journaling, painting or playing an instrument provides an outlet for emotions and fosters a sense of accomplishment. By including diverse activities, you will be addressing different aspects of your wellbeing, creating a balanced and satisfying routine.

Affirmations, as mentioned earlier in Chapter 10, can reinforce your positive beliefs and boost your confidence. In the evening, reflect on your daily writing in your journal, practice relaxation techniques such as deep breathing or taking a warm bath, and end with expressions of gratitude. This practice will help you focus on the positive aspects of your life, fostering a sense of satisfaction. Weekly routines may include therapy sessions, social activities with friends or support groups, and self-care rituals, such as a spa day or a nature walk. These activities will offer you opportunities for connection, support and rejuvenation.

Life is dynamic and your needs may also change over time. Therefore, you must be willing to change and adapt as well. Be open to adjusting your routine based on your current circumstances. If a particular activity no longer serves you, then replace it with a more beneficial one. Allow yourself to be compassionate when routines are interrupted. It's not the end of the world. It's natural to face interruptions, whether due to unexpected events or simply because you feel overwhelmed. Instead of being hard on yourself, acknowledge those interruptions and gently guide yourself back into your routine. Develop strategies to get back on track after these interruptions, such as setting reminders, creating a visual calendar, or seeking support from a friend or therapist.

A reflection session at the end of each week can also help you evaluate what has worked well and what needs adjustment. Keep track of it in your journal This practice encourages self-awareness and continuous improvement. Remember that the goal is to create a routine that supports your healing and growth, not to have rigid rules imposed on you. Flexibility and self-compassion are essential components of a sustainable and effective healing routine.

When you create a solid foundation for sustained emotional wellbeing, you are establishing a personalized, varied and adaptable structured healing routine. This routine becomes your reliable anchor for meeting life's challenges with greater ease and resilience. Remember that the healing process is continuous and that each step you take will bring you closer to a more balanced and fulfilling life.

STAYING CONSISTENT WITH SELF-IMPROVEMENT

When faced with various obstacles, it is difficult to maintain consistency in self-improvement and it can be an arduous task. One of the most common obstacles is the lack of motivation and commitment. It's easy to start with enthusiasm, but maintaining that momentum over time can be difficult. It's likely that one day you'll wake up feeling discouraged or wonder why you're struggling. Overwhelm and burnout are also major challenges in emotional development. When you try to do too many things at once, it will only lead to exhaustion and a sense of defeat. As a result, you will give up on your goals altogether. External factors, such as work and family responsibilities can further complicate this self-improvement process. These obligations will consume your time and energy, leaving you little room for personal growth. This is why it's crucial to celebrate any small achievements and milestones along the way. Acknowledge and reward yourself for every step forward you've achieved, no matter how small.

This positive reinforcement will help boost your morale and encourage you to keep striving.

Using the technique of positive reinforcement is the act of rewarding yourself to further increase your motivation, and they don't have to be extravagant rewards. Simple pleasures such as treating yourself to your favorite meal, taking a day off to relax or even buying yourself a small gift can be very powerful and effective motivators as these progress tracking tools can help keep you remain focused and accountable. Journals and reflective notebooks allow you to document your journey and leave a tangible record of your growth. Apps and digital tools designed for tracking habits can provide real-time feedback and reminders, helping you stay on track. Progress charts and visual checklists can also be effective. Seeing your progress visually can be very motivating, as it gives you a clear representation of your accomplishments.

The role that accountability plays in maintaining consistency cannot be overemphasized. That's why having someone to share your goals with can make a significant difference. A partner or support group can provide encouragement, support, and a sense of shared commitment. Similarly, regular visits to a therapist or coach can offer professional guidance and keep you aligned with your goals. Setting reminders and prompts for self-care activities ensures that you don't lose sight of your goals. These reminders can be as simple as setting alarms on your phone or using sticky notes in visible places.

Interactive Element: Tools for Tracking Progress

Consider using habit-tracking apps like *Coach.me* or *Habitica*, which offer personalized coaching and gamification elements to make habit creation more engaging and fun. Applications like *ClickUp* can also help set, track, and achieve your personal goals with features like Goals, Tasks, and customizable daily checklists. There are also journaling apps like *Day One* or even traditional paper journals for documenting your journey and reflecting on your progress.

Despite your best efforts, there will be times when consistency will falter. Life is unpredictable, full of unexpected events that threaten to derail even the best laid plans. When this happens to you, it is essential that you remain compassionate with yourself and understand that setbacks are a natural part of the process and not a reflection of your worth or ability. When you have faltered, don't be discouraged, but rather acknowledge it without feeling guilty and then refocus on your goals again. Flexibility is key here, as it allows you to adapt your routine according to your current needs and circumstances. If you find that a particular goal is no longer relevant or achievable, modify it to better suit your current situation.

Perseverance in self-improvement is a dynamic process that requires your patience, persistence and adaptability. With the tools discussed in this chapter, you can stay committed to your goals. Remember that the path to self-improvement is not a straight line, but a series of steps that, if taken consistently, will lead to significant and lasting change in your life.

CELEBRATING YOUR PROGRESS

It's important to acknowledge and celebrate your progress to stay motivated and confident in yourself. By recognizing how much you've accomplished and appreciating the positive changes you've made along the way can help reinforce good habits, positive behaviors, and changes. This recognition shows your brain that your hard work is meaningful and encourages you to keep pushing towards your objectives. For this reason, celebrating your successes can boost your self-esteem and sense of self-worth. Every little achievement is a reminder of your strength and commitment. If you recognize this aspect, you can shift your self-perception positively. Start enhancing your-self esteem in a significant way! Taking time to appreciate your achievements will help you stay continuously motivated and driven on your journey towards personal development and growth.

Ever time you celebrate a milestone, treat yourself with something special that you've been longing for? It can be as easy as spending a day by the sea, or treating yourself to your favorite meal, or that book you've been eyeing for a while now! And, don't forget to share your successes with your loved ones; it only adds happiness and joy to the mix!Sharing your successes with loved ones will build a network of support that cheers you on and enhances the joy of your accomplishments. Another effective strategy is to make a *vision board* showcasing your achievements by pinning notes or images to it that represent your milestones. This visual reminder will inspire you daily. And, writing about your triumphs in your journal will give you a chance to reflect and acknowledge the work you've put in to achieve your goals.

Remember that recognizing and acknowledging your progress is essential in nurturing an empowering atmosphere for your personal development journey. It not only uplifts your self-confidence and drive, but also nurtures a stronger bond during the journey of healing and self-discovery. Remember to cherish your accomplishments as you evolve and grow into the remarkable individual you are becoming... that person you were always meant to be.

CONCLUSION

*a*s you reach the conclusion of this journey and reflect on the path you've taken, look back on the progress you've made so far through this book – a companion guiding you to uncover, understand, and heal your inner child. Let's revisit some of the important aspects we explored in this book to ensure that these valuable insights remain with you as you move forward and progress in life.

We started by exploring the concept of inner child using personal anecdotes and historical background to understand how our childhood experiences affect our lives as adults. We discussed psychological theories from experts like Carl Jung, Roberto Assagioli, and Richard Schwartz to stress the significance of recognizing and addressing our inner child to deal with emotional and psychological struggles. We discussed about how guided imagery practices and self-evaluation tools can help individuals connect with their inner child and identify common traits or signs of a wounded inner child, such as insecurity and fear of abandonment.

Then, we examined the emotional baggage we all bear. Stemming from lingering childhood feelings such as guilt and shame that haunt us through our lives with impacts on our connections with others and our professional growth. We recommended methods like journaling to reflect on how our emotions and experiences affect our relationships, career, and overall wellbeing. We also suggested mindfulness techniques and therapy to release these pent-up emotions.

We emphasized the importance of acknowledging past childhood traumas as part of the healing journey. We identified common types of childhood wounds like emotional neglect dealing with abandonment issues and experiencing both physical and emotional abuse or mistreatment. Through real life stories of resilience and recovery shared in our studies, we discovered how people were able to move past these wounds. Our findings also highlighted healing methods such as communicating with your inner child through dialogues, utilizing Cognitive Behavioral Therapy techniques and embracing reparenting techniques to provide comfort and care to your inner self.

We discussed how the influence of the inner child affects adult decision-making and relationships and suggested activities such as self-reflection sessions and positive affirmations to improve communication with your inner-child.

Understanding and healing your inner child can result in making more conscious decisions and foster better relationships.

In the subsequent chapters, we focused on identifying unresolved trauma, setting healthy boundaries, managing emotional triggers, and transforming negative self-talk. Each chapter provided tools and exercises to help you go navigate these challenges. We introduced techniques like guided journaling, role-playing scenarios, and mindfulness practices that support emotional stability and resilience.

We also talked about how important it's to be open and honest in relationships, showing vulnerability and building trust to create deeper connections and emotional intimacy between people. We provided exercises to foster deeper connections and emotional intimacy and emphasized on how important it is to share your true self and embrace authenticity in order to achieve a fulfilling life.

We explored several holistic healing methods like mind-body practices, yoga, nutrition, and engaging in creative arts to help you improve both emotional and physical wellbeing, and provided exercises and tips on how to incorporate these approaches into your daily routine.

Finally, we underlined the significance of deep self-reflection and developing self-worth. We also discussed the Socratic questioning techniques, maintaining a reflection journal as well as practicing empowerment exercises, foster self-exploration, discovery, and individual development. We also emphasized the importance of making time to nurture your-self every day and acknowledge your achievements to sustain your healing progress.

The main lessons from this book are evident: recognizing and nurturing your inner child involves a life changing process that demands self-awareness and kindness toward oneself. Acknowledging past wounds and establishing boundaries while handling emotional triggers and embracing vulnera-bility can help you develop a stronger sense of self-worth and emotional wellbeing. Practicing holistic healing methods and regular self-reflection will aid in your continuous develop-ment and resilience.

Now, I encourage you to continue this journey of healing outside these pages of this book. Take the tools and strategies I showed you and make them a part of your daily routine. Remember that healing is an endeavor; and there's no harm in reaching out for assistance from therapists, support groups, and your loved ones.

Remember always that you're not alone in this endeavor; there are many others facing their own internal battles who are working for their emotional freedom form their burdens. Your dedication to personal growth and self-discovery demonstrates your courage and steadfastness when facing life's challenges.

To close, I'd like to share with you an inspirational message:

 You have the ability and power to heal, grow and transform your life. Your inner child deserves love, compassion, and understanding. With kindness and empathy towards your inner child, you're setting the stage for a brighter tomorrow. Embrace your journey with courage and grace, knowing that with every step you take, you are closer to wholeness.

LEAVE A 1-CLICK REVIEW

Customer Reviews

⭐⭐⭐⭐⭐ 2

5.0 out of 5 stars ▾

5 star ▓▓▓▓▓▓ 100%	Share your thoughts with other customers
4 star 0%	
3 star 0%	Write a customer review
2 star 0%	
1 star 0%	

See all verified purchase reviews ›

I would be incredibly thankful if you take just
60-seconds to write a brief review on Amazon,
even if it's just a few sentences!

https://www.champlinks.com/sl/InnerChildHealing-Paperback-Review/

ABOUT THE AUTHOR

Janet G. Cruz

With a robust academic foundation in Sociology and Psychology, Janet is deeply passionate about understanding the complexities of human behavior. She has authored several insightful books that aim not only to educate but also to offer practical strategies for overcoming addiction. Her goal is to contribute meaningfully to public awareness on issues related to mental health and societal well-being.

By leveraging her comprehensive knowledge and experience, she strives to foster a more informed and compassionate approach towards individuals struggling with addiction and other disorders.

She has also worked in the healthcare industry for many years and has firsthand experience with the challenges associated with caring for a loved one with dementia. Her passion to help others led her to write a series of books on dementia caregiving: a series of comprehensive resources for family and friends of those living with dementia.

She expertly blends scientific insight with personal narration to offer readers a comprehensive understanding of the relationship between the brain and recovery. Her mission with this book is to help others find hope, strength, and solace in their journey to healing. With her work, the author hopes to reduce the isolation and stresses associated with mental health.

She is the author of a variety of books in English and Spanish, such as The Dementia Caregiver's Guide,Dementia Caregiving, Guía de Supervivencia para Cuidadores de Personas con Demencia," "The Power of Communication Skills and Effective Listening: Say What You Mean and Mean What You Say," and "Developing Drug Addiction Recovery Skills by Understanding Addiction and The Brain: The Ultimate Guide to Build Resilience to Prevent Relapse," also available in Spanish, and many other books.

REFERENCES

Inner Child Work: How to Heal By Reparenting Yourself https://www.bigselfschool.com/post/inner-child-work

Inner Child Guided Meditation | Free Meditation Script https://mindfulnessexercises.com/inner-child-guided-meditation/

9 Steps to Healing Childhood Trauma as an Adult https://www.psychologytoday.com/us/blog/mindful-anger/201804/9-steps-healing-childhood-trauma-adult

Inner child https://en.wikipedia.org/wiki/Inner_child

What is Unresolved Trauma? https://www.verywellmind.com/unresolved-trauma-symptoms-causes-diagnosis-and-treatment-6753365

Recognizing and Treating Child Traumatic Stress https://www.samhsa.gov/child-trauma/recognizing-and-treating-child-traumatic-stress

Long-Term Consequences of Child Abuse and Neglect https://cwig-prod-prod-drupal-s3fs-us-east-1.s3.amazonaws.com/public/documents/long_term_consequences.pdf

The Importance of Personal Boundaries - Psych Central https://psychcentral.com/relationships/the-importance-of-personal-boundaries#:~:text=Boundaries%20can%20help%20you%20assert,be%20self%2Daware%20and%20independent

Assertive Communication: What It Means and How to Use It https://www.verywellmind.com/learn-assertive-communication-in-five-simple-steps-3144969

Self-Care 101: Setting Healthy Boundaries - Dana Nelson, Ph.D. https://www.dananelsoncounseling.com/blog/self-care-setting-healthy-boundaries/

4 Real-Life Examples of How to Set Boundaries https://thewellnesssociety.org/4-real-life-examples-of-how-to-set-boundaries/

How to Identify and Overcome Trauma Triggers https://psychcentral.com/health/trauma-triggers

30 Grounding Techniques to Quiet Distressing Thoughts https://www.healthline.com/health/grounding-techniques

21 Mindfulness Exercises & Activities For Adults (+ PDF) https://positivepsychology.com/mindfulness-exercises-techniques-activities/

Building your resilience https://www.apa.org/topics/resilience/building-your-resilience

Managing Your Inner Critic: How to Break Free from Judgement and Protect Your Mental Health https://www.hcbh.org/blog/posts/2024/january/managing-your-inner-critic-how-to-break-free-from-judgement-and-protect-your-mental-health/#:~:text=Constant%20judgment%2C%20especially%20towards%20ourselves,stress%2C%20anxiety%2C%20and%20overwhelm

How to Make Positive Affirmations That Actually Work for You https://www.wondermind.com/article/positive-affirmations/

Self-Compassion Practices: Cultivate Inner Peace and Joy https://self-compassion.org/self-compassion-practices/

Change the Internal Narrative by Confronting Your Inner ... https://thesciencesurvey.com/editorial/2023/06/06/change-the-internal-narrative-by-confronting-your-inner-critic/

Research. Brene Brown https://brenebrown.com/the-research/

Why Vulnerability Will Change Your Life: The Power of being yourself https://www.betterup.com/blog/vulnerability

How to Use Mindfulness Therapy for Anxiety: 15 Exercises https://positivepsychology.com/mindfulness-for-anxiety/

12 Proven Trust-Building Exercises to Repair Relationships of All Types https://riveroakspsychology.com/12-proven-trust-building-exercises-to-repair-relationships-of-all-types/

Efficacy of journaling in the management of mental illness https://www.ncbi.nlm.nih.gov/pmc/articles/PMC8935176/

Visualization for Post-Trauma Recovery - InnerGrowthCoach https://www.innergrowthcoach.com/visualization-for-post-trauma-recovery/

100 Art Therapy Exercises - The Updated and Improved List https://www.expressiveartworkshops.com/expressive-art-resources/100-art-therapy-exercises/

Role Play in Therapy: 21 Scripts & Examples for Your Session https://positivepsychology.com/role-playing-scripts/

12 Science-Based Benefits of Meditation https://www.healthline.com/nutrition/12-benefits-of-meditation

A Rapid Review Exploring the Role of Yoga in Healing Psychological Trauma https://www.ncbi.nlm.nih.gov/pmc/articles/PMC9741324/

Nutritional psychiatry: Your brain on food https://www.health.harvard.edu/blog/nutritional-psychiatry-your-brain-on-food-201511168626

Expressive Arts Therapy: 15 Creative Activities and Techniques https://positivepsychology.com/expressive-arts-therapy/

Socratic Questioning in Psychology: Examples and Techniques https://positivepsychology.com/socratic-questioning/

Using the Reflective Journal to Improve Practical Skills Integrating Affective and Self-Critical Aspects in Improvised International Environments. A Pilot Test. https://www.ncbi.nlm.nih.gov/pmc/articles/PMC8394420/

The Emotion Wheel: What It Is and How to Use It [+PDF] https://positivepsychology.com/emotion-wheel/

The coping insights evident through self-reflection on stressful military training events: Qualitative evidence from self-reflection journals. https://www.ncbi.nlm.nih.gov/pmc/articles/PMC10078775/

Why Self-Esteem Is Important for Mental Health https://www.nami.org/Blogs/NAMI-Blog/July-2016/Why-Self-Esteem-Is-Important-for-Mental-Health

Relation between childhood experiences and adults' self -esteem: A sample from Baghdad. https://www.ncbi.nlm.nih.gov/pmc/articles/PMC4344981/

Self-affirmation activates brain systems associated with self-related processing and reward and is reinforced by future orientation. https://www.ncbi.nlm.nih.gov/pmc/articles/PMC4814782/

99 Self-Care Activities That Can Improve Your Quality of Life https://www.goodrx.com/health-topic/mental-health/self-care-ideas-activities

Cognitive Behavioral Therapy (CBT) for Treatment of PTSD https://www.apa.org/ptsd-guideline/treatments/cognitive-behavioral-therapy

Revisiting the Origins of EMDR | Journal of Contemporary Psychotherapy. https://link.springer.com/article/10.1007/s10879-023-09582-x

Breathwork for Healing Trauma: 3 Popular Techniques ... https://www.othership.us/resources/breathwork-for-healing-trauma

Tai Chi Exercise for Mental and Physical Well-Being in Patients with Depressive Symptoms: A systematic Review and Meta0Analysis - NCBI https://www.ncbi.nlm.nih.gov/pmc/articles/PMC9957102/#:~:text=Tai%20Chi%20is%20an%20exercise,and%20reduces%20stress%20%5B23%5D

The Transformative Power of Structured Routines https://www.recoverlution.

com/knowledge/the-transformative-power-of-structured-routines-in-recovery

Personal Healing Plan: Prosper in Your Spirit, Soul, and Body https://uncagged bird.com/prosper-in-your-spirit-soul-and-body-with-a-personal-heal ing-plan/

10 Best Personal Development Tools to Reach Your Goals in 2024 https://clickup. com/blog/personal-development-tools/

Emotional Wellness Toolkit | National Institutes of Health (NIH) https://www. nih.gov/health-information/emotional-wellness-toolkit#

www.ingramcontent.com/pod-product-compliance
Lightning Source LLC
Chambersburg PA
CBHW071405120626

46546CB00002B/820